G000270882

For my mother

Losing I

# Losing Israel

Jasmine Donahaye

Seren is the book imprint of
Poetry Wales Press Ltd
Nolton Street, Bridgend, Wales

www.serenbooks.com
facebook.com/SerenBooks
Twitter: @SerenBooks

© Jasmine Donahaye, 2015

The right of Jasmine Donahaye to be identified
as the Author of this Work has been asserted
in accordance with the Copyright, Designs
and Patents Act, 1988.

ISBN 978-1-78172-252-7
Mobi: 978-1-78172-253-4
Epub: 978-1-78172-254-1

A CIP record for this title is available from
the British Library

All rights reserved. No part of this publication
may be reproduced, stored in a retrieval system,
or transmitted at any time or by any means
electronic, mechanical, photocopying, recording
or otherwise without the prior permission
of the copyright holders.

Cover image: Shatta village, 1933

The publisher works with the financial assistance
of the Welsh Books Council

Printed by CPI Anthony Rowe Ltd, Trowbridge

# Contents

*...Water me and nothing else,*
*water me. Beauty won't do, love won't do, God won't do –*

*even this life won't do, nor any life. Water me,*
*I am thirsty.*

Amir Or, *Poem*
translated from the Hebrew by Helena Berg

*Ond mi wn i am brofiad arall sydd yr un mor ingol, ac yn*
*fwy anesgor ... a hwnnw yw'r profiad o wybod, nid eich bod*
*chwi yn gadael eich gwlad, ond fod eich gwlad yn eich*
*gadael chwi, yn darfod allan o fod o dan eich traed chwi,*
*yn cael ei sugno i ffwrdd oddiwrthych, megis gan lyncwynt*
*gwancus, i ddwylo ac i feddiant gwlad a gwareiddiad arall.*

J. R. Jones, *Gwaedd yng Nghymru* (1970)

# Proem – leaving Israel

I live in a wet place. My old stone house, a smallholder's *bwthyn*, once thatched, now slated, once whitewashed, now bare stone, is at the bottom of a valley, between a stream and a river, which used to be a ford across the road. I've lived here twelve years, but the house stands as it has stood for at least two and a half centuries, the wall built in places into the rock. It used to have *Fferm* attached to the name; a woman called Jane Williams lived and died here and was the last to farm its land; then it changed hands, the land was sold, and the house became a home only to people, not to animals whose warmth used to rise from the barn at the lower end and heat the living quarters. The barn is gone, knocked down to accommodate a wider road; there are ruins of a pig and chicken house; the stream has been rerouted and piped under the field, and the course it used to take is dry in the summer, like a wadi. But it doesn't want to flow that way. When it rains hard, the stream breaks its bounds and bursts up out of its pipes to rush down the hillside by the house, spreading out and making a wide shallow river of the garden, flooding towards my doorway, swirling around the porous stone walls, washing away mortar, seeping in and swelling the plaster.

At its worst, after days on end of falling rain, when the river is in flood, when the culverts can't take the run-off, and the stream is tearing around the house, when the ground is pulpy and swollen, I feel I might go mad with the surfeit of water, and I think of desert and burnished sky, the smell of eucalyptus, the call of a palm dove, and I am ready to move, to go back to Israel, to engage, even though, whenever I'm there, I can't wait to leave.

Sometimes I think Israel is gone from me. After I came back from a long summer there, in 2009, I went out onto the peat bog near the autumn equinox. It was empty of dogs and people, of men pointing with authoritative knowledge at birds. The days were turning cold, and the midges and mayflies were gone. The blackberries were waterlogged and maggot-ridden after a summer of torrential rain. The bog is a place of waterways, once treacherous, then drained so that the peat could be cut and stacked and dried for fuel, and now reflooded to preserve what's left of a wilderness that was almost lost.

In the soft mud of an open space beside the walkway were otter prints so fresh it seemed they had just been made, and the softening blurred prints of a bird. I went there once in the company of a man with whom I believed myself to be madly in love. It was before the signposts, before the boardwalk and bird-hides and woven willow screens. There was only the overgrown path of the disused railway line, and perhaps we went through a gate, ignoring a *no trespassing* sign, or a warning, and ventured out onto the bog along a narrow raised plank path encroached by reed and bog-cotton and dark water. The planks were surfaced with the remains of a rusty netting to add a little grip when the wood was wet and slippery. We walked to the river and stopped on a low rail bridge to watch the swell of the water towards us. We both saw and pointed at the same time to a line of bubbles across its surface – knowing and yet not daring to know what it was, because the bubbles cut across the current. They were not a result of the water flow against something submerged, but the sign of an otter, which broke the surface of the water and looked at us looking at him. Lazily, not finding what he saw to be of interest or something to fear, he turned and swam away around the bend and out of sight, and the man I was with said, 'Right, let's go home,' and I said 'That's it?' and he said, 'I think we've seen what we came for.'

When I came back alone at the equinox, it was cold but clear, and I sat down on the wet boards to be out of the wind and to wait for whatever I had frightened to feel safe again and emerge. Off in the distance a marsh harrier was quartering the sullen remnants of a field where the farmer had given up cutting or ploughing the reeds; it put up a flight of startled mallard, which it ignored. Then they dropped back down and settled. Everything went still but the slight wind sibilant in the purple grass and reed.

I lay down on my back and looked at the sky. On the horizon dark cumulus was building, ponderous with rain that would be shaken loose when the clouds reached the high slopes of Mynydd Bach, near my house. I felt my keys slide towards the opening of my pocket. There were gaps in the boardwalk. I thought that if the keys slipped through I might never retrieve them. I would be adrift, alone. For a moment I thought this was how I wanted to die – by walking untrammelled and unremarked into a wild place and lying down and letting the world slip away. I remembered years ago feeling that in the Negev Desert, feeling its immensity and impersonality. I was driving north through the desert with my younger daughter towards Be'er Sheva, the city of seven wells. The first indications of habitation were the camel crossing signs. They're valuable animals, and some owners mark them with fluorescent paint so that they will show up in your headlights when you're travelling the unlit desert road. After the camel signs, the outermost straggle of the city was the Bedouin villages and camps, their black tents and corrugated tin roofs, and then on the horizon the familiar urban forms appeared – industrial towers trailing plumes of smoke or steam, highrises: Be'er Sheva, ancient and modern.

We stopped in the city to see a friend, Eitan. The heat was extraordinary, but Eitan said, 'I have something to show you,' and he took us out of the air-conditioned cool of his house and along a few blocks of dusty streets and pale stone walls to the British military cemetery. The grass was wrong – thick-bladed, sharp, hard – and thin feral cats and sandy stray dogs were slinking away in its shaded borders, but otherwise this cemetery was like all British military cemeteries: row upon row of pale headstones, and in this one, row upon row of Welsh names. These were the young men left behind in the desert during General Allenby's push from Gaza to Jerusalem nearly a century ago, when Lloyd George asked him to capture Jerusalem as a Christmas present for the nation in 1917.

I don't know why it moved me so much, those Welsh boys, many of them from the villages around where I now live, lying forever in that land which their own country mapped onto itself as an image of holiness and lineage. At home in Wales I drive everywhere through a landscape marked by Hebrew names.

In the cemetery in Be'er Sheva, the Welsh boys lie surrounded by streets onto which modern Israel projected its own ancient and recent military history: HaMacabi and Bar Kochba, HaPalmach, HaHaganah and Ha'Aliya, 'Street of the Return', every inhabited place an invocation of the past as a legitimisation of the present. And as in every Israeli city, there are streets named after its great literary and cultural heroes, too – Bialik, Bezalel, Yehuda HaLevi... I thought of the graves of those Welsh boys killed in 1916 and

1917, lying in quiet, pale, stone ranks in the British war cemetery in Be'er Sheva, as I lay in the silence of the peat-bog, making a fantasy of death – a death without pain, or lights, or anyone's care; a life and an ending to it adrift in the world, untied.

But we aren't usually given deaths like that. They are messy, and involve other people. When my sister died seven years ago I could not stop weeping. It was as though she unleashed all the grief I'd felt for years; I became a child, abandoned, desolate, sobbing and inconsolable. I still cannot think of her dead and not weep. I had not known she was ill until three days before her death, and then came my father's call to say she'd died; then I was travelling to London, weeping on the train, weeping at Heathrow airport, breathless, light-headed, wandering in shock for four hollow hours in the airport in Hong Kong on the way to Australia for the funeral. A week before her death I had walked across the peat-bog with that man, seen the trail of bubbles that heralded the otter, but now that too was gone; he'd passed through for the last time.

You can't repeat moments of splendour; you can't return to them. Even my sister's death had about it a kind of splendour – there was a hard purity in her determination not to let the fears of others ignite her fear, and in her belief and will that she could be cured intact, without the butchering machinery and crude poison of modern medicine. There was, in its way, a kind of splendour in grief, too – our terrible emotion in the garish light and noise of subtropical Queensland; my parents raw and open for the first time, and the aftermath, when, back at home and alone in Wales, I felt everything wrung with misery. But you can't live in that kind of intensity for long; it calms, or you calm down, or retreat. You remember it, and each return to the memory entails a small loss of feeling, a blunting and a forgetting. Grief quietens, as does splendour, and you become a voyeur, looking in on your own memory.

This is what happens every time I leave Israel: there is an unreality, as though I cannot quite adjust from full colour to partial colour. The continual jostling of the present and the past, of omissions and concealments, of alternate names and stories with their injustices and outrages, is simultaneously enlivening and exhausting. It is always a relief to leave, but always, as soon as I have left, the homesickness starts up, a longing to go back. It's a homesickness for a state of mind as much as a place – this intense, contorted, alert conscious-ness, a kind of hyperreality.

You can't live like that though; it is only intense for me because I am there for short periods. Living there, outrag-eous conditions become normalised. A girl paints her mother's nails as the two of them wait to go through a checkpoint. A woman with morning sickness retches into a pink plastic bag waiting while a soldier compares her with the photograph in her ID. In Hebron, if you're Palestinian, you need a strong wire-mesh screen in order to sit on your balcony. All the time you know what's happening in Gaza, but you acclimatise and become immune to it because you have to get on with a drab daily life of work and family, paying the next bill and worrying about the new noise in the car engine; but also, perhaps, you become immune because you can, because it's easier, because you choose not to question the accepted narrative of security and threat, because you choose not to see – because you feel helpless to change what you see, because you are tired, so tired, you can no longer care. Yehuda Amichai wrote about Jerusalem that it is

... full of tired Jews,
always goaded on again for holidays, for memorial days,
like circus bears dancing on aching legs.[1]

But it's not just Jerusalem. Most of Israel is tired. Goaded, most Israeli Jews perform, but they are tired of the performance – the secular ones, anyway. And I got tired, too; I chose not to put on that costume and dance. Instead I left. I always leave. And now, perhaps, at last Israel is leaving me.

# 1 – Motherland

It is the year of clogs and flared skirts, of shiny striped shirts with big collars, the year the PLO infiltrates by boat on the coast north of Tel Aviv and takes a bus-load of passengers hostage. It is spring, 1978 and I am ten years old. Security at El Al Airlines is high. I know the names Abu Nidal and Abu Jihad and Leila Khaled – Leila Khaled, that woman who is somehow not really a woman, but a terrorist.

Israel is an impression of barbed wire and rusting yellow warning signs on the beaches, the scent of orange blossom and the stink of sewage, hot nights and ruins – and a huge sprawling network of strangers who are relatives. It is my mother's first return home after fifteen years of self-imposed exile, and it opens in me a wound I can never heal – a longing to come home to a place that can't be home.

Now whenever I return, it is the long straight road through the valley to the kibbutz that catches at me – after Afula, that dusty way-station; after the last turnings, where it straightens out into the old Roman road that runs through the Jezreel Valley or the Plain of Esdraelon or Marj Ibn Amer, depending on your political orientation, or language, or biblical inclination. 'The Ruler Road' my mother called it, that first time we went back in 1978. The mass of Mount Gilboa rises on your right, and far off in the distance there's a shimmering above the road where the border lies, some twenty kilometres away. Beyond it rise the Jordanian mountains, the mountains of Gilad or Gilead, after which my grand-father Yair named himself and my family – *Hagiladi*, a man of that place. On either side of the road stretch the fishponds, where you can see white-fronted blue and chestnut Smyrna kingfishers, and pied kingfishers and black-winged stilts; and then, looming up under Gilboa, the complex of the prison moves into sight, watchtowers and barbed wire topping the long external wall, which runs alongside the dusty road. A short distance beyond the prison a trilingual green metal sign points out the left turning to the kibbutz.

Through every return, the kibbutz lies like a magnet at the centre, exerting a force that pulls each journey into a curve inward to its core. Even now, after I have learned its other story, it exerts its pull. This is where my mother is from, and so I have always felt that this is in some way where I am from, too. No matter what I learn about its history, what I feel about its government's acts, its citizens' electoral choices, what I think about its political foundations and exclusions, Israel is inextricably caught up with my mother – my inaccessible, elusive mother, who left her community and her country, but inwardly never left, who carried her home all the years of my childhood not in a book, as some anti-Zionists will say the 'true' Jew does, but in the locked chamber of her heart.

My mother was born in Palestine in 1941, in the hospital in Afula, the dusty town on the road to Beit She'an, or, in Arabic, Beisan – it was, in 1941, an Arab town. The British Mandate still had seven years to run before the last dignitaries and soldiers and diplomats would board the final ship from Haifa and leave the Arabs and Jews of Palestine to fight it out by themselves. Kibbutz Beit Hashita, the communist settlement in which she grew up, was established in 1935, halfway between Afula and Beit She'an. Her parents were friends; they had worked as contracted labourers together at the salt works, because there was not enough work yet on the kibbutz; they had married, and within a year had separated, while my grandmother, Rahel, was still pregnant with my mother. Later, Rahel had become involved with a married man, and had been compelled to leave the kibbutz, so that my mother, growing up in the small, closed, starkly conformist community, was always part outsider. Later, when her mother used to come back to visit, it made her feel like one of the non-member children who lived there as a type of boarder.

My mother, like all kibbutz children at the time, was brought up in the children's house. The children would spend a short time each afternoon with their parents, but otherwise they lived under the care of the *metapelet*, the children's nurse. The communal raising of children relieved women of the burden of parenthood and enabled them to take part in kibbutz life as equal members, with equal status – or that was the belief. In the Freudian Marxist thinking of the early kibbutz movement, being kept away from close proximity to their parents' neurotic inclinations meant that children would be relieved of the bourgeois burden of an Oedipus complex. In a hardline kibbutz, where the ideology was most exact and absolute, a parent might make a point of greeting the other children before their own when they met them walking along a path, so that there could be no question of preferential treatment. Beit Hashita was a hardline kibbutz.

My mother left Israel with my father in 1963, when she was twenty-two, and she did not return from England for fifteen years. By the time she went back to visit, the Six Day War was more than a decade in the past; less distantly, the Yom Kippur War had almost been lost. She returned to a transformed country, a country massively expanded, with

West Jerusalem forced back into unhappy unity with its eastern half, now annexed and made into the new capital; with the tamed heights of the Golan, which had once threatened above the tiny frontier kibbutz of Gadot, where she and my father, years before in the late 1950s, had done their bit to try to people the border, and failed; and with the great expanse of the Sinai and the great scoop of the West Bank filled in.

Over the weeks leading up to the Six Day War, my parents had followed the build-up on the borders on the tiny black-and-white television screen in their cramped flat in Twickenham. They clung to each other in anxiety and mutual reassurance. My mother wrote to her family in Israel. None of them had telephones, and she had no news. She wrote about my brother, Guy, and his talkativeness and about my sister, Illana, who had started to walk; about the progress of my father's studies, and her acquisition of careful BBC English, but she never mentioned her guilt about leaving; she never mentioned her homesickness.

Each night during the escalation, after my brother and sister had been put to bed, after my mother wished them *halomot metukim*, sweet dreams (as, later, she would wish me every bedtime, so that my night-times were threaded with the unmappable geography of Hebrew), she went into the tiny living room, and with my father sat down to watch the nine o'clock news, my mother peering, short-sighted, at General Nasser's familiar face, railing, filling the screen.

Every day, haltingly, she read the newspaper from cover to cover, standing lost in the news, her arms holding the paper wide, as she still does, while my sister napped in the early afternoon. During the late afternoon she would take my brother and sister to the playground. My brother's English by then, in 1967, was becoming fluent; it had been more than two years since he'd stopped speaking Hebrew. One Saturday morning, a heavy older boy, the plug of mucus in his nose crusted with sand, had stood over him and told him to get off his swing. My brother had looked up, blank and uncomprehending, so the boy had pushed him off. My mother realised then that she would have to switch to English. Like so many Israelis, my mother had grown up with only one language, despite generation after generation of Jewish multilingualism. Without any idea of the riches and possibilities of bilingualism, alone in her mother-tongue, she gave it up. By the time I was old enough to remember, my brother had lost his first language, and Hebrew had been reduced to family secrets and dreams. It lingered only as a private language between my parents, and in my bedtime rituals.

Now over the days the suspense built and built. Perhaps I was conceived in that suspense. Perhaps my parents gave each other some comfort, and what started me was an easing of their distress. Night after night they watched the reports of troops manoeuvring, tanks massing; night after night they heard the calm, reasoned BBC interpretation of angry polemic. Then Israel acted, and their unbearable suspense and anxiety shifted from the potential to the actual.

Certainly for my parents this was a necessary pre-emptive act. To them, the Israeli bombing of Egypt's fleet of MiGs, those gleaming metal toys lined up, vulnerable, wavering in the heat rising from the tarmac, was the trigger of a war that was going to happen anyway. They could not countenance the other version, that it was an act of aggress-ion, that Israel provoked a war that otherwise would have remained merely manoeuvres and rhetoric. Those airfields lay orderly and still on the morning of the 5th of June, 1967, before the Israeli airforce tore out of the Negev, screaming like the Harriers and Tornadoes that rip through Welsh airspace, causing sheep to abort and women to miscarry. Compared to the romance with the air in these names, how utilitarian the Russian numbered jets seem – MiG-17s, or MiG-21s.

During the six days of the war, my parents' anxiety focused, narrowed, became not a calculation of risk, but a calculation of potential success, and then of actual success. Perhaps my first cellular divisions were not marked by uncertainty, but instead were flooded, irradiated by relief, then joy, then euphoria. This was how Yitzak Rabin's widow, after his assassination, remembered the outcome of the Six Day War: 'This euphoria,' she kept repeating; 'this *euphoria*.'

Maybe that's when I began, a collision of cells in a flood of euphoria. It's what I grew up with: Israel idealised, heroic, embattled and honourable, powerful out of necessity, and always moral in its deployment of power. It's what I held onto long into my adulthood, only slightly troubled by the changes in others' views. But underlying my parents' fierce relief, bounded by moral rectitude, as they believed then, was my mother's homesickness.

Homesickness, and the longing for return, saturated my childhood. My mother's yearning was palpable. Later, when a poem that I wrote about it was published, she asked, 'But how did you know?' How could I not have known? Her homesickness was like the unhealing, unhealable wound of the Fisher King. When I read that, in some children's version of *Le Morte D'Arthur*, or *Gawain and the Green Knight*, or *Parsifal*, and, later, found it redacted in Susan Cooper's *Silver on the Tree*, where the mournful, grieving king has been wounded by doubt, I recognised it instantly – how the king begs to be left alone, his voice full of an aching sadness. But though in the end he is relieved of his despair, for my mother there was no such comfort.

That first time my family went back to Israel, in 1978, I hadn't wanted to go. I was afraid of being homesick. I suffered terribly from homesickness. If I went on a school trip, if I went to a friend's house, I became distressed – I missed the safety of my mother. For the first two years of school I wept at the window, watching my mother leave, or wept when, having got absorbed in something, I looked up to find she'd gone. I was painfully, totally attached to my mother. Even when I was with her, I missed her, because part of her was always missing – part of her was inaccessible, is still inaccessible, lost inside the cold, hard lock-up of her soul, which the kibbutz exacted from every child as the cost of the ideal, new, egalitarian society.

My parents coaxed me into excitement about travelling to Israel through the promise of new birds. When I was nine years old, all my being was focused on birds. Wherever we went, I ordered places by birds: I navigated by the birds I had seen and the birds I might see. For my ninth birthday, my father had given me the massive *Birds of Prey of the World*, which I still have. I pored over the *AA Book of the Road*, with its illustrations of the great-crested grebe's mating dance, and the coloured, precise cross-section of a green woodpecker's head, so you could see how its ant-adapted tongue coiled inside its skull. I saved pocket money for months to buy the chocolate-brown RSPB *Birdlife of Britain*. Now my father let me look through his precious first edition of Henry Baker Tristram's *Fauna and Flora of Palestine*. Tristram had a string of letters after his name – LLD, DD, FRS. The pages smelled musty, and the heavy book was old, very old, from long ago in the previous century. There were protective wax papers over the coloured plates, and taxonomic divisions and Latin names I could not understand. I turned the pages carefully, reading Tristram's odd, old-fashioned descriptions of griffon vultures, and sunbirds, and the grackle, which was named after him, and we spent hours together with the Collins *Birds of Britain and Europe, with North Africa and the Middle East*, identifying and listing what new birds we might see: the roller, the bee-eater, the hoopoe, bulbuls, Smyrna kingfishers, eagles and wheatears. That battered copy, published in 1972, which my parents have kept all these years, is marked, throughout, with a little inked Star of David, for each species we saw during that month-long trip in Israel in 1978, and the next in 1980, and their later return visits without me, after I'd left home.

My family had moved from London to a village in Sussex when I was a year old; when I was seven we moved again to a house on the edge of Ashdown Forest, where we went birdwatching at the weekends. We travelled to Wales in 1973 and 1974 looking for red kites, and we drove a long car-sick journey through fields and stone walls until at last we came upon a pair of them floating out of the mist somewhere near Tregaron, a sighting that even now, when he describes it, makes my father's voice reverently hushed. In France we saw flamingos and golden orioles, a bird so glorious and odd with its cat-cry that for a while I adopted Oriole as my middle name. Often on Sundays we would go birdwatching at Weirwood Reservoir, rushing there, once, when we heard an osprey had been sighted. For three months, for a Young Ornithologists' Club competition, I got up at dawn every day to make a record of the wildlife in a small patch of wasteland and woodland at the edge of the A22. There is a mound there, planted with ancient yews, and riddled with badger setts. It is the old midden of the nearby manor house, but we called it the burial mound and every spring, when the badgers cleared out their setts, I looked in the fresh heaped earth for bones. I knew the common British birds by silhouette and flight pattern, by their gait or their call; I knew the birds I had not yet seen from the books, and from a scratchy record of the dawn chorus I listened to over and over.

None of this birdwatching could compare to the teeming wealth of birds I saw, at ten, in Israel. Israel was, for me, a landscape known first through its birds. The birds, and my excitement over them, my absorption in them, was also a refuge, because during this first visit, and the subsequent one, my mother, rediscovering and revelling in her own language, became a stranger.

It begins in the aeroplane, as we land. We are given sweets for the landing, and when the plane touches down, a drift of voices begins to sing, and my mother sings too, quietly. It is a melancholy, haunting melody I've not heard before, and I look at her, shocked: she is wiping her eyes under her glasses. I have never before seen her cry. Later, when I learn it, *HaTikva – The Hope*, the Israeli national anthem – and even now if I hear it, it is that moment it evokes: the shock of uncertainty, my mother remote, caught up in feeling something I cannot understand but immediately want to be part of, and my sense of alienation from her, of loss, and yearning.

We walk down the metal stairs and the evening is purple and velvet and warm, and men are kissing the dusty tarmac at the foot of the steps, repeatedly, mumbling, in a kind of passion.

In my grandmother's seventh-floor apartment in Tel Aviv, I wake up the next day, weeping. In Hebrew, my

mother is transformed and unreachable. Unable to understand her, I see her clearly: simultaneously familiar and
unknowable, like those around her – people who look like
her, black-haired, olive-skinned, who look like me, too, but
with whom I cannot talk.

It is my tenth birthday, and I want to be home. My
mother's mother is enormous and loud. She frowns at me as
I stand there crying, and asks something about me in
Hebrew. She sounds annoyed. I go out on the balcony and
look down at the small patch of garden far below. Something
is moving there – some brown bird. I can hear the ritual
shouts of officers and soldiers being drilled over in a nearby
military camp. I hear the long wail of sirens, a different
sound from the seesaw of the siren that I know, usually the
village constable getting home in a rush through traffic for
his lunch. My father has said something about air-raid sirens
– the night before he had to explain, patiently, that these
were not air-raid sirens but police cars or ambulances.

Seven storeys down, the tiny square of dusty green
garden is hemmed in on all sides by the tall apartment
buildings, which squat on great concrete legs, and I think I
might ask if I can go down to look for birds, but my mother
calls me in for breakfast. This is a return of surging unhappiness: breakfast is nothing I recognise as a meal. It is
chopped tomatoes and cucumbers, different kinds of white
cheese, and yoghurt, and cream cheese, hard-boiled eggs…
The milk, poured from a plastic bag, tastes foul, like long-
life milk. My grandmother eats with her mouth open,
making wet sounds and sucking her teeth.

I meet my grandfather for the first time when we travel a
few days later up the coast and inland, onto the Ruler Road
and past the prison, past spur-winged plovers and Egyptian
vultures, to the kibbutz.

The lenses of my grandfather's glasses are so thick they give him an amused look, as though his eyes are half-closed in private laughter. We smile at each other a lot but can't speak: he has no English and I have no Hebrew. There is a great healed scar on his forehead, from when he was attacked and wounded by Arabs. I know it is Arabs who did it, though no one tells me that. His scar fits with everything I have been learning about 'the Arabs'.

He drives a small tractor with a trailer, and dresses in the dark blue work-shirt and shorts that all the kibbutz members wear, and the *kova tembl*, the fool's hat, to shield himself from the sun – it is early April and already hot. In the communal dining room where the adults sit for long hours, talking, my sister and brother and I fidget, uneasy and bored. People in their blue work-clothes keep coming over to us; there is a lot of exclaiming and kissing. My father is no longer Daniel, but *Danny*. My mother – it hurts me, what has happened to my mother. In Hebrew, incomprehensible, her eyes bright, talking, with people listening to her, she is transformed. I am used to her quietness, her hesitations, her looking to my father to speak. Now it is for the first time my father who is in the background, my mother who is sought out and addressed and kissed, excitedly. These people talk to me brusquely, and kiss me too, and I can understand nothing. I look to my mother for help, but there is some new quality about her that I can't bear: she is animated, nearly loud, emphatic. I hate it – I want her back. I hate everything: the loud and crowded communal dining room, the smell of bleach and old wet food where the wheeled orange dish-trays clank along the conveyer belt into the dishwasher, and the hot-bleach smell of the steaming cutlery coming out of the dishwasher. Everyone talks loudly; everyone wears blue shirts and trousers and dark heavy boots. In Hebrew everyone seems angry, even when they are laughing.

My sister and I scrape our plates and load our dishes onto the conveyer belt and go downstairs and out from under the ponderous concrete edifice of the central dining room. Even the grass is wrong – thick-bladed, coarse, dry, though it is green. We balance, wobbling, along the narrow wall by the road, our arms spread. Out here passing people stare at us – prolonged stares – but don't speak. We see pale jays, and hoopoes, and yellow-vented bulbuls, and a small dark bird that might be the tiny, green, iridescent, orange-tufted sunbird.

We spend weeks that spring bird-watching, with my siblings and I competing for the binoculars – the heavy black pair that I can hardly hold, and the lighter brown pair belonging to my mother. My brother is more interested at fifteen in other novelties. My mother, alarmed, smacks his hand down when he looks through binoculars at an army camp. We travel throughout Israel, seeing members of my mother's and my father's families, some of whom, on my father's side, have only recently escaped, with difficulty, from the Soviet Union. We visit sites in the West Bank, which, under Jordanian control, were inaccessible to my parents when they left in 1963. We travel north into the Golan, and to an aunt's kibbutz in the Huleh valley; we go to see ancient Jericho, and the ruins of Caesarea and Masada. In the Old City in East Jerusalem, we enter the Dome of the Rock, and shuffle forward in a queue to touch the stone, smoothed into cool silkiness. It makes me thirsty, somehow, in the back of my throat. We drive south to Eilat, and into the Sinai Desert – far south along the Red Sea, in what used to be, and subsequently becomes once again, Egypt. The car breaks down several times, or overheats.

Everywhere we go, it is not family, or ruins, or human stories that make the strongest impression on me, but birds. Masada is a bird-of-prey migration, not a site of heroic Jewish resistance to Roman rule: short-toed eagle, spotted eagle, imperial eagle, honey buzzard... The raptors rise on the thermals from the Negev and float past us at eye-level. On the broken walls of Masada there are lines of Tristram's grackles, large dark birds with orange wing feathers and a haunting cry – Tristram's grackles, spelled *grakle* in his *Fauna and Flora of Palestine*. Beit Hashita, the kibbutz my mother is from, is Smyrna kingfishers and black-winged stilts with red legs, and hoopoes. The Sinai is wheatears, every species of wheatear, and griffon vultures circling, and perhaps a black vulture – and white beaches, and an occasional Bedouin, and the car overheating, and white branches of hard, dead Red Sea coral, which we collect, illegally, and smuggle home wrapped in clothes in our suitcases.

For my mother, birds were a simple delight, but it was different for my father. When I was a child, my father was the bird authority. He had the collector's condition, which had begun as a boy, when he'd gone bird-nesting with his twin brother along rural hedgerows, after they were evacuated from London because of the Blitz. But the mark in a book, the addition to a list – those birdwatcher acts of reduction and ownership weren't important to my mother. When I was very young and my siblings were at school, she and I would take binoculars and walk up alone through the orchard and the field and in among the high deciduous trees of Ashdown Forest. The forest was a bit of wild and ancient Sussex, hiding remnants of charcoal burning and royal boundary markers. Alone, between the two of us, there was a quiet intimacy. That spring we found the downy round nest of a long-tailed tit. For weeks we watched it woven, and occupied, but when we came back from Israel it was empty. And one time, walking under ancient deciduous trees, we heard the unmistakable call of a wood warbler, and then saw it, brilliant yellow-green, flitting through the thin branches of a stand of young oaks. When we told him, my father made a moue of doubt, but we were resolute. My mother's certainty was the only small rebellion against my father's confident bird authority that I recall.

We walked throughout the forest, its broad old beeches and oaks, its heaths and firebreaks, and each part of it was marked by birds: the red-legged hobbies in a stand of Scots pine, tiny goldcrests in the cedars, a blackcap in the clearing near the old midden, and the long-tailed tits' nest we found in the great tangle of brambles growing over a long-ago fallen fir. In the woods and fields, and working in the garden, my mother was at home in herself, and the clench of homesickness and unhappiness on her would lift. Birdwatching with her in those wild wet places was intimate and intensely private. She was so much part of me, I was hardly aware of her. So when I saw her for the first time transformed, alien and inaccessible in her first language, the attachment tore, and I became aware of myself, separate and alone. Israel had always kept part of her from me, but when I was ten, Israel took her back entirely, and I was bereft.

Two years on, and it was not birds but boys who came into focus. In Israel for another month-long visit, I noticed for the first time young Israeli men, and soldiers. I was twelve, and I watched them intently. Dusty, in uniform, an M16 or an Uzi slung over one shoulder, they lounged in bus-stops, like film-stars smoking harsh cigarettes down to the burning filter which they held turned into their cupped hands. Dark, unshaven and rough, most importantly they were romantically tragic, subject to extreme experience and damaged by warfare. I was sharply jealous of my brother, who, unlike me – and lazily uncaring about it – was a *sabra*, a Jew born in the land of Israel. Sabra, the native prickly pear cactus, is the image of the New Jew, the tough Israeli, prickly and rough on the outside, but sweet on the inside. After 1967 this became the image of the ethical, emotionally sensitive Israeli soldier who shoots and cries.

How I longed for that erotic combination of brusque rudeness and sweet tenderness. Spending months in Israel at twelve, and without my parents or siblings at fourteen, and fifteen, I, too, wanted desperately to be a sabra; I wanted to belong, to be what my mother was, to be whole. The green quiet of Sussex, the birds of Ashdown Forest – all of it faded into dullness before the passion of exile and return that I discovered. England had been nothing but a temporary resting place, I decided; in an adolescent embrace of the idea of homeland, I believed I had never really been part of anywhere but Israel.

I did not know yet that *sabra* meant something very different, too; that it was an Arabic word, and its place in the landscape, green and spiked and sprawling, was not wild and accidental, but meaningful, the sign of another story, half-erased but still visible – if you knew to look. As a child and a teenager I was given no hint of that other story, hidden and contradictory. Instead the woundedness of the Israeli soldier enthralled me. I wanted not only to be a sabra, but to be wounded, too, to be damaged and tender and resolute.

The national story is simple, full of dusty guns, of hopeless courage and miraculous delivery, of connection to soil and to deep history. Israel offered the possibility of being cleansed of all that was suddenly wrong about being Jewish – because according to this story I was being told, the Jews in the Diaspora, in exile, were homeless and helpless, persecuted for their ethnic and religious differences wherever they went, wherever they lived. Unlike the cowed, weak, pale, nationless, hand-rubbing, demeaned Jew of the Diaspora, victim of antisemitism, speaking Yiddish and wearing sagging braces (the Yiddish and the braces twin shuddering horrors for my mother), the New Jew in Zion was tall, straight, muscular, tough, and above all, proud – a worker of the land, wielding gun and pitchfork and red flag, and singing bright, heroic songs. This was what I might do, too; this could be me, if I chose – because, though surrounded by powerful enemies intent on their destruction, and fighting alone for survival, the New Jew had prevailed and was redeeming the land, creating a just, democratic, benevolent and *moral* society for all citizens, and for all Jews worldwide.

This was my mother's heritage and I understood it to be my own heritage, too. The kibbutznik was the ideal – not an effete intellectual, nor a mean usurer, but a noble, enlightened peasant, once again rooted in native soil. According to the kibbutz version of the Zionist story, the return of Jews to this mostly empty land to redeem and restore the waste and desert to their former glory as fertile fields, was heroic in a socialist rather than biblical sense. My grandfather, peasant-kibbutznik, became for me its embodiment: he too had wielded flag and pitchfork and gun; he too had worked with his whole body, his whole being to create a new society, to realise a dream. He was a worker of the land, weathered by harsh sun, idealism and labour.

At twelve, I learned and embraced this national story, Leon Uris's *Exodus* version of it. From that stirring romantic novel, from the places we visited, from family, from newspapers and, later, from film, I absorbed the simple, compelling Zionist account of the past and present, and of my past and present. This was the version, not much more sophisticated, which was reinforced when, at seventeen, I thought I might move to Israel permanently, and came under the formal influence of the Jewish Agency.

My father had done it before me, along with his twin brother, in 1956: he entered Israel as a new immigrant and joined the army. When he emigrated from England at the age of twenty-one, he had been galvanised by the story of Israeli independence, like so many Jews in the immediate aftermath of statehood, and he too had wanted to help 'build up the land'. It was a mere eight years since the 'miraculous' war of independence, and the Jewish Agency, burdened with the task, after the war, of bringing Jews to Israel, ran language immersion programmes for new immigrants on many of the kibbutzim. These Hebrew ulpans consisted of six months' intensive immersion in Hebrew, and induction into the Labour Zionist ethos of the kibbutz movement. Six days a week, the new immigrants studied for half the day, and for half the day they worked – in the dairy, the factory, the kitchens, the citrus groves, or the fields.

My mother was sixteen when my father turned up with his guitar and his handsome laughter, and she was shy. At the beginning the members of the kibbutz viewed him with suspicion as a dangerous Western capitalist influence, because of the guitar. Their romance was a kibbutz drama. Even now, when I meet old kibbutz members for the first time, it is that romance that they remark on when they learn who I am. My father worked in the *refet*, with the cows.

Later, after he'd finished his three-year army service, he and my mother moved to the small frontier kibbutz of Gadot, up near the troubled, dangerous Syrian border.

That my mother left the kibbutz of her birth at all was a betrayal, an abandonment (she was a *bat-kibbutz*, a daughter of the kibbutz). That she then left the kibbutz movement for a city life was worse, but that she and my father finally left the country altogether, so that he could continue his studies in England, was, in that coercive society of personal and collective responsibility to the state, the worst form of national treachery. Now people come and go, but at the time the social sanction against leaving made it a taboo; it tore a hole in the fabric of the national myth.

In contrast to the heady term for immigration, *aliyah*, with its meanings of ascent, as to a holy place, to emigrate was to 'go down' – to descend into the pit of diaspora. My mother was a traitor, and she knew it. It lingered and festered like a curse. She had been afraid to go back. She had been afraid of censure, and it had taken fifteen years before she could face it. And then, when at last we had gone back, she had been embraced – everywhere we went she was embraced, and welcomed. All of us were; all of us were enjoined to return permanently, to be again part of the family.

When we returned to England that second time, my mother was pregnant. I had been the youngest of three, and the news about my imminent displacement made me anxious and then jealous and unhappy. In the autumn my mother spent long weeks in hospital with high blood pressure. I refused to visit her – the hospital was an hour's drive away, in the small rural hospital in Cuckfield. I told my father that the drive would make me car-sick, but it was because I could not bear to make a fact of my mother's absence by seeing her elsewhere. I could not bear it that she was pregnant either. I pretended nothing was happening, that nothing was changing, and when it did change, when my mother came home with my new baby sister, Rowena, I told my parents I wanted to leave them, to leave England, to go back to Israel, to the kibbutz, to live. By then, at the age of thirteen, I had completely absorbed my mother's unreconstructed Labour Zionism, taking in the kibbutz ideology by which she was formed and making it into a romantic idealism. I was attached to it; I defined myself by it and I took refuge in it from this new unhappiness. But though my parents considered it, in the end they would not let me go. Although I accepted and then came to love my new sister, my mother remained inaccessible: at first she was taken up with my sister's care, and then she fell ill. My adolescence became a dark tunnel, and four years later I dropped out of school and left for Israel after all.

I was seventeen, impressionable, and ripe for the Jewish Agency's nationalist story in its most overtly propagandist form. Like most of the people on my kibbutz ulpan, I didn't know if I was running away from something or towards something. The kibbutz where I was placed wasn't very old; it had been established after 1948 on the site of a depopulated Arab village by Jewish immigrants from north Africa – but we knew nothing about that. It was 1986, and we knew almost nothing about Palestinians. The kibbutz was very poor, one of the poorest, and it was a highly dysfunctional community, riven by family feuds, and without a clear identity.

Because I was the daughter of a kibbutznik I was welcomed not as a possible new immigrant, a new recruit to the national body, but as a wayward kibbutz daughter returning to the fold. Through the medium of the ulpan, the Jewish Agency tried to persuade us degenerate, western, Diaspora Jews to *return*, and I, easy prey, understood that I could repair the breach, could heal the wound created by my mother's abandonment: I could undo that betrayal by my permanent return. The national story was my own story; the collective was my collective. My roots were deep, deep and ancient, and the path from the Jewish past to the Israeli present was uncluttered and simple and linear.

We were taught that Jews, dispersed in Roman times, when the Temple was destroyed, had always longed to return to their ancestral home, intoning at every Passover 'Next year in Jerusalem' as a matter of course. Some, over the intervening two millennia, made the journey back. Now we could, too; in fact we had a moral duty to do so.

Leon Uris popularised this simple narrative in his immensely successful propagandist novels *Exodus* and *The Haj*, which I had read voraciously as a young teenager, caught up in their melodrama. There were tents in the sand, treachery, the flash of daggers, the gleam of teeth in the darkness, men who could move silently, women who were pure and lovely. *Exodus* was outrage, glory and Hollywood technicolour in the person of Paul Newman. *The Haj* was more complicated. Purporting to tell the 'other story', it was partly narrated by a village mukhtar's son whose masculinity was questionable, a cleverly undermining conceit in the muscular, brash, frontier-novel tradition of Wilbur Smith, to whom Uris owed a great debt in style and attitude. I read Wilbur Smith's novels too – South African adventure stories for white men, in which women were loose and dangerous and got what was coming to them, or pure and to be protected; modest and shy, desire had to be coaxed reluctantly out of them, and then they often died. Smith's books always seemed to feature a tough, white, male hero and a noble, exceptional and impossibly divided chief who tried to rise above the limitations of his hopelessly primitive culture. So did Uris's *The Haj* – in his case, a tough Jewish hero and a noble, exceptional mukhtar. The leaders of these bloodthirsty people – Zulus or Matabeles, in Smith's books, Arab fellahin in Uris's – were always doomed to fail.

The message of *Exodus* and *The Haj* was unambiguous: when the Jews began to arrive in Palestine, the Arabs, what few there were of them, were backward, ignorant and uncultured. They barely scraped a living from the land; they were variously nomads or peasants (but not like the enlightened, idealistic peasants of the kibbutz movement). Besides, most of them had arrived from other areas of the former Ottoman Empire only after the Jews had begun to create new economic opportunities in the wasteland that was Palestine. They identified, if they identified at all, as Arabs, in a pan-Arab collective, but they were tribal rather than national in their affiliations, and disunified and squabbling. The Arab was weak, exploitable, and subject to irrational passions. The Jew, by contrast, was righteous, developed, civilised and moral. And we Jews had a right, an ancestral right much older, deeper and more meaningful than that recent and tenuous connection claimed by Arabs in Palestine. The Arabs could go anywhere in the sprawling undifferentiated mass of 'Arabia', but Jews had nowhere to go but the Land of Israel.

*The Haj* reinforced everything I had been learning, without words, about 'the Arabs'. The mukhtar was rapacious, oversexed; the women were frightened and stupid; boys would go after their own sisters if they could. And they were responsible for their own catastrophe. The

Arab uprising of 1936 was bloody and vicious and under-
hand, and all the Arabs of Palestine under the leadership of
Al Husseini were in cahoots with Hitler. During the Second
World War, the Arabs were about to sell out to the Axis
powers, and then all the Jews would have been slaughtered;
there would have been a double Holocaust. After the UN
voted for the partition of Palestine in 1947, the Jews were
nobly willing to accept far less than they needed or wanted,
but 'the Arabs' in their folly and short-sightedness refused
it. So when the British withdrew and Israeli statehood was
declared (legally, it was always stressed – because of the UN
Partition Plan), the new, vulnerable, tiny state ('tiny' was
important: it was always David against Goliath) had to
withstand the unprovoked attack by the armies of seven
Arab countries, intent on its destruction, innumerable in
their troops and much better equipped than the heroic,
hastily formed Jewish people's army with its few dusty guns.
And tiny, embattled Israel prevailed, because it couldn't
afford not to. Because we had nowhere else to go.

On our kibbutz ulpan, the Jewish Agency gave us the same
story, the same bracing and exciting message. We travelled
in pairs to Jerusalem to participate in a history and Jewish
identity workshop; we were taken on tours to Yad Vashem,
the holocaust museum, and to Masada, site of heroic Jewish
resistance to the Romans. We were courted, and encouraged
to make the grand decision to *return*, to become Israeli.

Throughout it all, in what we heard and read and saw, the
word Nakba was never spoken. What happened to the
Arabs in Palestine from 1947 to 1949 was a footnote to the
story, an unfortunate by-product, and their own fault; it was
certainly never accorded the status of its own special term.

According to the Zionist version of events, after the declaration of independence and in the course of the war (started by the Arabs) some of the Arabs fled; they were ordered to by the advancing Arab League and Transjordan's Arab Legion, and they were promised they could return to the whole of Palestine cleared of Jews. They were afraid (of course they were afraid, we thought – they were Arabs), and they were gullible and misinformed. But the Jews never threatened, only defended; the Jews were civilised and moral soldiers. Everything that happened to the Arabs was a result of the Arabs' own doing. They were betrayed by their own. And one could never trust their numbers; they were nothing but propaganda. 750,000, nearly 800,000 refugees? This was double the number who really left. And what about the Jewish refugees from Arab countries whom Israel absorbed and resettled? This cancelled things out, in a population transfer like that of India and Pakistan at Partition. At the same time, the Jews were nearly annihilated, nearly pushed into the sea – but so desperate, so lacking alternatives, so much love did they have for their land, that they risked all, and won. And then plucky little Israel for the next sixty years withstood enmity and the threat of annihilation, and redeemed the land – making the desert bloom, building cities and planting gardens, creating a new, just, democratic, independent state in which Jews could for the first time in two thousand years live as free citizens, proud of their Jewishness, taking their place in the world of nations.

In 1986 we were still a year from the start of the first Palestinian uprising, and it was still possible to believe and to claim that there had been no such thing as Palestinian nationalism before the 1950s. Sure, there had been Arab group *feeling*, but 'Palestinian' as an identity was an invention, like the PLO, after the fact. Hadn't the Jews themselves been Palestinians before Israeli statehood? The Palestinian refugees were an invention used by the Arab countries: never allowed citizenship or assimilation, always promised the imminent return of 'their' land, always used as tools and bargaining chips, they were forever being exploited. In 1986 it was also still possible to believe that those who had come under Israeli control after the Six Day War nearly twenty years earlier enjoyed much better conditions than those they had suffered under the Jordanian and Egyptian occupation which had preceded Israel's control. Under Israeli rule of the West Bank and Gaza, Palestinians had local government, universities, schools, hospitals… What more could they want? Any real concern the Palestinians had could be dismissed as ingratitude. Conveniently, they were represented by the Palestine Liberation Organisation: its members were busy taking hostages and blowing up aeroplanes and generally reinforcing the idea that you could never trust an Arab.

But there was the beginning of an unease in 1986 – a demographic one. Palestinians in the Territories had been reproducing more quickly than Jews – even more quickly than the prolific reproductive systems of religious Jews. It was beginning to look as though with the West Bank and Gaza part of Israel, Jews would soon be outnumbered, and how then might Israel be a Jewish state?

Even after the start of the Intifada, most of this unambiguous, emotive national story that we were offered remained unchanged, retaining its grotesque exaggerations, convenient omissions and grandiose claims, its fragments and false emphases and downright lies. The package came complete with a flag, a powerful ancient symbol, a language reborn; it told a tale of heroism and idealism, and of courage in the face of adversity. Most stirringly, it came with a melancholy, sweet national anthem. And though the Jewish Agency made a great deal of the Holocaust, my family story was not a Holocaust story, and for me it was the socialist version of the Zionist narrative that resonated: my mother had been a worker, rooted in the land. Every May Day the kibbutz flew the red flag, and my mother in pigtails and kerchief had marched with her young comrades, singing the *Internationale*.

How could I resist, at seventeen, the power of the claim to such a past and such a present? How could I resist the power of that welcome, that embrace? My past was the admirable, kibbutz-peasant past. I knew who and what I was; I knew where I was from – and it all led back to my ever-present, ever-absent mother.

The first time I spoke to my mother in Hebrew, there was a look on her face, in the hesitation before she answered, of nakedness. It felt like a transgression, this entry into who she was that was not possible except in her first language. It shocked her. It shocked me too. For one unguarded moment her deep past, her buried childhood rushed up in her and responded, and I witnessed it; for a brief moment, before she once again guarded herself, there was an intimacy I had never before known. And then it was gone. Now, if we speak in Hebrew, she laughs away her own rusty vocabulary and old-fashioned grammar. She has been out of Israel more than twice as long as she lived there. She is happy, and settled, and in her seventies, but I am still driven by this sense that part of her is absent and inaccessible, stolen by the kibbutz when she was very young; and that part of her could never be expressed, because she was always an immigrant, and never in her first language. Her sadness, alone in the children's house, and her unhappy homesickness all through my childhood and adolescence, has made me and shaped me. It has attached me to her, and, through her, to Israel in ways I can't seem to undo.

The kibbutz experience is a damaging one. It is only recently that people have begun to acknowledge the effect on children of the communal experiment. Studies have examined kibbutz children's psychological attachments, their ego formation, but in published oral histories, kibbutzniks who were raised collectively reveal the fear, the sadness and the loneliness they experienced in the children's houses. They remember crying in the darkness; they remember wetting the bed because of their terror of going to the bathroom in the night, and they recount the false promises of the *metapelet* that their parents would come, though their parents never came. For many parents, too, it was traumatic to be separated from their children when they were so young, but at the time, within the kibbutz movement, to question a fundamental social organising principle like the collective raising of children was to risk being labelled a bourgeois reactionary.

My mother, raised by a *metapelet*, became one as an adult, working in the children's house in Kibbutz Gadot up on the Syrian border, where she and my father had gone after he finished his military service. Later she fed my brother and sisters and me in the strict four-hour intervals that she'd learned then; we all cried ourselves to sleep, and eventually stopped crying. That's how I fed my first daughter, too. I, too, let her cry herself to sleep, though it troubled me to do it: it's what I learned from my mother.

I didn't know about my parents' first child, stillborn when my mother was eighteen, until I was a teenager; I didn't know until long afterwards about my mother's sense of failure, the requirement to carry on as though nothing had happened. The harsh discipline of stoic toughness started at birth.

My sister, unnamed, unmarked, made the sixth generation of my family to be buried in that dusty corner of the former Ottoman Empire. It is an odd, disorientating reversal to realise that my other sisters and I are the first members of the family to be born and to live elsewhere in many generations, to see us suddenly as an anomaly in more than a century of settled community. The hole my mother tore by leaving Israel is not a notional one. Nor is it a matter of fantasy to say my family are Palestinian Jews. They have lived for more than a hundred and thirty years in that place – the first on my grandmother's side arriving in Ottoman Palestine in the 1880s, and on my grandfather's side in 1914.

Is where you're from where generations of your family are buried? I no longer know, and perhaps it doesn't matter. The graves of your ancestors don't bestow belonging, or moral rights – but they do engender feeling. This is where my mother is from, though she left. Israel, and more particularly Kibbutz Beit Hashita, is where my grandfather is buried, and my great-grandparents beside him. It's the only place I know of in the world that generations of my family lie buried; it is the only place I want to be buried, too.

As with any national narrative, in order to legitimise itself, the modern Israeli one is grafted, like a new fruiting variant, onto an old gnarled trunk with deep historical roots. The claim of deep history happens at the national level and at the level of community and settlement and family, and at the level of the individual, too, but the scar of the grafting remains – and the scar makes denial about the past impossible. Of course I have lost faith in the simple Zionist story, however much it used to give me a sense of place in the world. What thinking person cannot be suspicious of a simple national past? There is no simple, singular national past – only an imagined one, composed of embellished facts and fantastical narratives, of retroactive hopes and deliberate omissions and reductions.

My family is implicated in that place with its wounds and scars and stories, both visible and invisible, and therefore so am I. Whatever our putative deep roots, I can never return to the romantic fantasy about the past that I had when I was a child and teenager and a young adult, a comforting fantasy of innocent belonging, but it still calls to me, that folktale; those archetypes still resonate. I can reject it, this grafted story, because of the moral wrong that it entails, and call myself a Palestinian Jew instead, but it doesn't change how I feel towards my mother's land.

My mother won't go back, but I wonder if I'll ever stop going back, in search of her, in search of myself. The cheaper flights arrive in Ben Gurion Airport at four or five in the morning. Each time I wait in the warm dark humidity of the train station for dawn, for the first train into the city. I absorb the new-old language around me, in the voices, and the announcements. There's always gum on the platform, and a warm smell of garbage, of acid and decomposition, and something spicy and sharp – a flowering tree, or its sap. My body's stance begins to adjust, to incorporate the gesture of the place, to take in the feel of its language again: to sense its way back to what is familiar, but also made new each time.

And always, every time, I want to kiss the dirty ground as those men did at the foot of the aeroplane steps some thirty years ago, my first time here, and *HaTikva*'s melancholy returns to mingle with my melancholy. Israel's national anthem is in minor chords, saturated with longing for a redemption that cannot be, a hope that cannot be fulfilled, because who can ever be fully at home in the world when that home rests on the homelessness of others? I could not be at home there – but I wonder if I can ever fully be at home anywhere else.

# 2 – Disorientation

In the year before Tel Aviv's centenary, large parts of the city are loud with construction. The first modern Jewish city, Tel Aviv was founded in 1909, but the neighbouring port city, Jaffa, now coerced into uneasy cohabitation, is, by comparison, ancient. Parts of Jaffa too are being redesigned in the lead-up to the centenary celebrations. In the old quarter it is spotless, the mottled pale stone pavings rubbed smooth by centuries of footsteps, the densely packed, small, stone buildings and narrow alleys and archways a network of boutiques, art galleries and jewellery showcases. But all the time in the background rage the saws and shouts and crash of construction.

It is thirty years since I first encountered this place, its noisy chaotic shuk, blind beggars rattling a coin in a tin can, all part of the story that told me where I was from. Now, at the age of forty, I have lost most of this story of the past, and – though I know it's a cliché – I have come back, as lost Jews often do, to try to figure out who and what I am.

My young cousin Klil has offered me a place to stay, a base without obligation or expectation – he neither feeds me, nor calls me for an account, nor rearranges his life for me, and in turn expects nothing from me. His apartment building in Jaffa has been condemned; outside, the street has been torn up for the new light railway, but he's not been evicted yet.

Each morning I go out into the heat and traffic of Sderot Yerushalayim where it runs past Old Jaffa, and walk through the market to Abulafia's for a pastry, and on up to the square for coffee. I pass the enclosed courtyard of an empty house that rustles with an endlessly agitated colony of fruit bats, wondering each time who it belongs to and why it is uninhabited. The tourists don't arrive until midday, and in the mornings the square is deserted except for one man setting out napkin dispensers and salt shakers on the cafe tables, where I sit with coffee, wondering how I have come to be here again.

I know the risks: reverently touching the ancient stones of Jerusalem's Old City, or visiting the Western Wall, or seeing the outrage of the Qalandia checkpoint – epiphanies of Messianic fervour are two a penny here, but even so, to return again seems a compulsion, something I can't resist.

Any crisis can serve as an excuse for a Jew to head off to Israel – the end of a relationship, loneliness, middle-age angst, grown children leaving home, a health scare, a death, or the confrontation with Palestinian trauma. Any one of these alone can act as a trigger, and I have had versions of all of them in quick succession.

My story of the past has been sloughing away for years. Though I resisted for a long time, I am no longer in denial about the 'other' story, about the cost of Israeli statehood and what it was based upon. For years I took refuge, first in California, where Jewish identity is uncomplicated and my sense of Israel remained largely unchallenged, and then in PhD research in Wales, where the country's past use of Israel as a model, its romantic nationalism, and the predicament of its endangered but resilient language all were resonantly familiar and exciting. Moving to Wales and engaging with its troubles was a form of Zionism displaced, a love of Wales-as-Israel. But Israel was changing, had already changed, had never been what I'd thought it was, and therefore that was true also of Wales. The story I was telling myself and telling others about the past, about my place in it, could no longer fit. All that I learned about Israel, and about the Palestinian experience, all that Israel's behaviour at home and in the world forced me to confront, left me confused and unsure of myself. I amended and adjusted, but nothing fitted together anymore; everything I might say was qualified, defensive. Then I discovered my own family's culpability in the displacement of Palestinians in 1948, and, profoundly disorientated, my sense of who I was came undone.

*Disorientated*, we say, meaning unsure where we are in the world, and, without a sense of where the east lies, unable to work out how to get where we wish to go. I have always had a dangerously poor sense of direction: it means I am always getting lost, sometimes with dramatic consequences. When I was nineteen I got lost in Jerusalem, by chance ran into the friend I'd been looking for, but in a different part of the city, and, driven in part by the apparent fatedness of our meeting like that, married him, had children and moved with him to the US. I was just nineteen when that began. I know how dangerously off-kilter Israel can make me; I know it's a risk to come here at forty, disorientated, at a point of crisis. Long since divorced, my daughters nearly grown, my sense of self in question, without much reason to be in one place or another, I want something momentous to take me over: all of who I am is up for grabs.

It was my grandfather's wound that changed everything – or, rather, a story about his wound, his scar. I was sitting in the late summer sunlight on the doorstep of my cottage, talking on the phone to my mother in Australia. My older sister had moved to Queensland years before, and after my father retired, my parents followed her, along with my younger sister, in 1999. In the background to my mother's voice I could hear raucous unidentified bird-life; in the background to my voice she could hear a soporific wood-pigeon, an indignant wren alerting everyone to the presence of a cat. Like this we had sat and talked in horror through the vicious wars of the previous summer – the Gaza war and then the Lebanon war of 2006. A year later I'd taken my younger daughter to Israel for a month, and now back home in Wales I was passing on to my mother messages of love from her sisters and her brother, telling her the family news, and anecdotes about our trip.

I'd visited my grandfather's grave in the cemetery at Kibbutz Beit Hashita, and my aunt had told me a story about how, when he was attacked and was recovering in the hospital in Afula, Shlomite, my mother's *metapelet*, had gone to see him to let him know how my mother was. At the time, everything the kibbutzniks possessed was owned collect-ively – they neither had their own clothes or shoes or furniture; they did not claim a bed or a room as theirs, but my grandfather kept a few personal items in a tin under whichever bed he slept in, and he asked Shlomite to keep it for him. This was how he and Shlomite got to know each other. Not much later, they married.

This story was new to my mother – that it was she as a very young child who had brought her father and his second wife together. It was a strange moment, sitting in the sun in Wales in the late summer of 2007, talking to my mother in the noise of Queensland's subtropical rainforest, about her father's hospitalisation in 1944 which she could not remember. I had never known who had attacked him, or why, and when I asked her, I realised how odd it was that it had never occurred to me to ask before. Uncomfortably, though not fully acknowledged, I knew the reason: it was

'Arabs' who had attacked him, and that had explained everything sufficiently. Carefully liberal elsewhere, where Arabs were concerned I was deeply and unconsciously illiberal: 'Arabs' in Israel had been to me an undifferentiated mass of hostility and danger, all actual or potential perpetrators of violence. I hadn't thought about individuals, about individual stories; I had always understood the assault on my grandfather as part of a common and generally expected Arab disposition towards Jews. That realisation was disturbing: it made me squirm with shame.

My mother hesitated before answering. 'It was Arabs,' she said, eventually. 'One of the skirmishes. You know – there were always skirmishes.'

'Yes, I know,' I said. 'But who? Where were they from? I mean, were they workers? Or from the prison?' Sometimes the kibbutz had hired Arab day labourers to work in the fields; sometimes inmates from the nearby prison had worked there, too.

'Well, I suppose people from the villages,' she said.

There are no villages near the kibbutz. The Ruler Road leads past the fishponds, with their ospreys and kingfishers, past crop fields and citrus groves, and cotton fields. Near the entrance to the kibbutz the shallow sewage treatment ponds spread out, waded by black-winged stilts and avocets. Further down the road there is the prison in its razor wire and watchtowers, and beyond it, on the other side of the road, lie other kibbutzim – Ein Harod and its sister kibbutz, which split off during the Communist schism of the fifties. Beyond them, to the west, towards Afula and north-west towards Nazareth there are some Arab villages and towns, and others further off in Wadi Ara, but I could not think of any Arab villages near the kibbutz.

'Which villages?' I asked. 'Do you mean near Afula, or

Wadi Ara?'

'Oh, I don't know,' she said. 'Yubla, probably, or Al Murassas.'

'Where are they?' I asked. I could not recall having seen Yubla or Al Murassas.

'Well, they're gone,' she answered.

'What do you mean they're *gone*?'

'I mean they're just rubble. You can't see anything now. Everyone left.'

'They left?' I said. '*When* did they leave?' But already, creeping in on me, was the certain knowledge of her answer.

'Oh, you know... In 1947, 1948. It was near the graveyard – beyond the graveyard. We used to go walking there, I remember. But the houses were already ruins. Or at least there were no roofs. Everyone left.'

What I knew about the Nakba I knew in a broad, general sense. Even though I had learned a little bit about this other history, about people fleeing their homes in fear, I knew and didn't know, just as many Jews, many Israelis, deliberately or otherwise, know and don't know. The details of *who* and *how* and *where* are passed over or sidelined in the ongoing argument about *why* people left, about what created the Palestinian refugee 'problem'. There are exceptions, like the massacre at Deir Yassin, although I had never heard of Deir Yassin as a child or a teenager. In many ways it is the argument over such extreme cases that has allowed the particular stories elsewhere to be lost in the broad generality of the term 'Nakba' or the 'War of Independence'.

There is no sign of those villages on a modern map of Israel. There are no signs naming the ruins and remnants of those villages in the landscape, either. You would have no reason to know they had ever been there. They have been erased from the land, and wiped off the map.

Now, hearing my mother name these two villages, Yubla and Al Murassas, it seemed obvious that there would have been villages near the kibbutz that were depopulated in 1948, and it shocked me that it hadn't before occurred to me. Nobody I knew or had met had ever referred to them before, yet here was my mother casually identifying two villages not as notional places, but as part of her childhood landscape, her childhood world. And it wasn't just Yubla and Al Murassas, as I was to find out later. A whole network of interconnected villages that had once spread out through that valley was now gone.

'Where did they go, then, the people from these villages?' I asked.

'I don't know,' she said. 'The West Bank, probably. Or Jordan. I don't know.'

When, earlier, I had learned in a general sense about Palestinian Arabs fleeing the threat of war and then fleeing war, about villages being destroyed to prevent their return, and to erase their memory, I had been outraged, and am still outraged. Nevertheless, there was always something detached about my reaction; it was always an outrage that had happened somewhere else. But here it was close to home, not in the abstract: here it was near Beit Hashita, in the place my mother came from. What had happened there? How had it happened – and how was it that I could not have known? All the many times I'd visited the kibbutz, all the long weeks and months I'd spent there, nobody had ever mentioned the villages. I'd never heard them spoken about, never heard the story told – and hearing nothing, knowing nothing, I'd never had a reason to ask. And now that I'd asked, now that the question had been asked, it could not go unanswered. After that revelation, everything realigned, and I could no longer maintain my last vestiges of denial and self-protection, believing (because I had wanted to believe) that all that was wrong with Israel had somehow happened elsewhere, had been perpetrated by other people. But it hadn't been. My family, my grandfather – my gentle, idealised, socialist kibbutznik grandfather – was implicated.

In Jaffa, sitting in the morning heat over coffee, the smell of bleach still lingering on the newly wiped tables, I wonder what, precisely, I'm now after. Shortly after the confusion caused by my mother's revelation about the kibbutz past, and the implications of that revelation, came new shocks and losses: my older sister, suddenly dead of cancer I had known nothing about; my uncle dead soon after; one of my daughters suffering an emergency lockdown at her high school in California, because of a gunman on campus. A mad love affair with an exquisite man ended; another connection with a damaged man left me empty and full of mistrust. I too had a cancer scare, though it turned out to be nothing at all, but it left me mistrustful of my body.

In Australia for my sister's funeral, I saw the birds I'd heard in the background of phone conversations with her and with my mother and father. The birds' raucous noise began at four in the morning and it was cacophonous: lorikeets and cockatoos and more garish overgrown things I had not heard or dreamed of. My parents and younger sister took me walking in lush wilderness – down a steep track to the rammed-earth house my older sister and her fiancé had just finished building, surrounded by untouched rainforest. There were fever-carrying ticks, and down at the waterhole we put up a king snake – it came whipping across the water towards us, intent. In the rainforest catbirds mewled like lost children, and wherever we went we could hear the sound of the whipbirds, the tense rising whistle of an imminent strike, and then the crack of the whip, two birds in a call and response of one violent whipcrack.

There were harsh confessional moments that only shock and sharp grief could allow to surface – about family silence, about lies told for good intention or ill, about omissions. The night before I left Australia to go home to Wales, my parents gave me the family photographs – the blue album my father's mother had put together in 1950; the small black-and-white photographs from the kibbutz; the glossy, square, garishly coloured Kodak prints from our visits to Israel in the seventies. They dug out birth certificates and marriage certificates, and my mother gave me my great-grandmother's gold brooch, which spelled out her name, Yafa, in Hebrew.

When I got home I pinned my parents' marriage certificate to the wall. Its paper is off-white, with a blue leaf-pattern border. Below the grand header of the Israeli Ministry of Religion, the Hebrew lettering is rounded, old-fashioned, the figures of the dates and the identity numbers carefully formed. In her black-and-white passport photo, with its scalloped white border, my mother is wearing a sleeveless dotted dress. Smiling, smooth-skinned, her face looks open and naked. She's not squinting, but without her glasses I know she can only see a blur. My father's photo is smaller, face-on; there is a hint of a suppressed smile. He's wearing an open-necked white shirt, and his hair is untidy. The date is 6 October, 1959 and my mother is eighteen years old.

Though my parents never registered my birth with the Israeli embassy in London, my mother's identification number confers on me Israeli citizenship. Any Jew, and anyone with at least one Jewish grandparent, can apply for citizenship, but this number is all I need if I want to get an Israeli passport: I am already a citizen. Or that's what the embassy told me, when I rang to enquire. They sent me forms, and I have them still. I have never filled them in.

My sister died in late September. After a week in the wildness of raw family shock, and the brash loudness of Queensland, the cool mistiness of rural Wales was disorientating and hauntingly melancholy. It was darkening, and the summer birds had left. Each day I drove along a back road to my job in the nearby town, through flocks of finches rising off the crumbling, ice-damaged tarmac, where they gathered to peck at the fine gravel. The hawthorn was dark with berries the colour of old wounds. The sheep had been taken down off the upland fields for the tupping season, and were kept in for lambing. In their place, the uplands were full of redwings and fieldfares, feeding on the fields and on the hawthorn and bright rowan. A buzzard huddled on a telegraph pole every mile. I always drove the back way, meeting no traffic, crying.

My sister dying, my uncle's death shortly after, my daughters far from me and vulnerable – the cumulative shocks made me a little crazy and raw. I began to think about giving up my safe civil service job at the Welsh Books Council, of moving on, of leaving altogether. The place I thought I'd made for myself in Wales felt tenuous, temporary – I wondered if there was any more reason to be there than in Sussex where I'd grown up, or California, where I used to live. Everything about my life felt in question. The shock of my sister's sudden death lasted; six months on it began to turn into a dragging sense that nothing would be worth doing again, that I was alone in a chilly, empty world.

Now that I am back in Israel, I am not sure which shock

has driven me here – the search for some new sense of place in the world, or wanting to find out about Al Murassas and Yubla. I' wonder if I am complicit in something deeply wrong, whether I have been complicit by loving a country whose government does wrong, whose very existence is based on a wrong. I think I might find out and perhaps try to tell the story of people who lived there in the Jezreel Valley near the kibbutz before they were displaced or driven out by the kibbutzniks. If I succeed in finding out, I hope I might do something good or right – but I know, really, that I am doing something entirely self-interested, perhaps as all good intentions are, because I am lost. Being back in Israel has disorientated me further. Everything I understand about it is in suspense – it does not offer me a sense of place, or a sense of direction, or a way to navigate: instead it shimmers with duality, and falseness, with things not said.

*Harus*, the map says – destroyed. Again and again, printed over in purple Hebrew – *destroyed... destroyed... destroyed...* Al Murassas: *harus*. Yubla: *harus*. Kafra: *harus*. Wadi El Bireh: *harus*. Al Hamidiya: *harus*. Jabbul: *harus*. Kawkab al Hawa: *harus*. It's a composite map, printed by the Israeli government in 1955, the landscape of that year superimposed on a trilingual British Mandate map from 1945, showing clearly what happened in the seven years following the start of the Arab-Israeli war in 1947. I was given a copy of it by Zochrot, an Israeli NGO that seeks to uncover, publicise and memorialise the full scale of the Palestinian Nakba, the Catastrophe of 1948. It's a palimpsest, a deep map, showing the location of features and resources important to British Mandate control in 1945, overprinted by what is important to the young Israeli government in 1955:

the aftermath of depopulation and destruction.

The Jezreel Valley section of the map details the network of spidery unpaved paths and roads that used to connect the villages. It records the oil-pipe, the overhead cables, the railway, water-courses and springs, and the paths along which people rode horses or donkeys, or walked carrying water and grain and children. These paths used to link all the villages in the valley near my mother's kibbutz, Beit Hashita: Al Murassas, Kafra and Yubla, Wadi El Bireh, Al Hamidiya, Jabbul, and Kawkab al Hawa, and in turn connected them to the towns of Beisan and Haifa, Afula and Nazareth. Now these villages are all gone. Above or below the name of each of them *harus* is stamped in purple Hebrew letters. The population was expelled or fled, their houses and holy places and schools were knocked down or blown up, and their wells were blocked with rubble, but the signs of the villages are still there on the map, as is the record of their destruction.

Once you know about it the landscape is transformed. Nothing you thought you knew can be trusted; everything is a sign for something that is missing, or a lie, or a story that you can't quite read.

My reassuring picture of the innocent kibbutz, the safe ground of my family roots, that place of birds and dust – the spruce-shaded cemetery which my grandfather landscaped and where he and his parents lie buried; the painful memory of my mother transformed and strange in the brutalist concrete central dining room with its clatter of trays, its swallows skimming in through its wide open windows, and sparrows hopping along the tables – all of it was some kind of centre for me, a place in the world by which I navigated. Now, learning about what has not been said, about what is not acknowledged, all that I have felt about the place is suddenly suspect. What I thought I knew has been turned inside out. And this place will never look the same again: it will always shimmer, everywhere, disorientating and confusing, with duality, and with the duplicity of its past.

I finish my coffee and wander down to the seafront. Here an earlier redesign that Jaffa underwent is evident in the potted history of its tourist information board. In the Israeli version of events, the town was 'liberated' in 1947. At Ben Gurion Airport, a plaque on the wall honours those who died there in the 'liberation' of Lod in 1948. I never before noticed the word 'liberation', but now the word and its strange jarring new duality seems to be everywhere, though it was always here – East Jerusalem, above all, 'liberated' in 1967.

Once you start looking, you can't not see it – you can't not look. Once you start asking, it is only by a huge effort of denial, a decision not to pursue it, that you can stop, that you can return to the safe knowledge of your old story, in which you have a place, by which you can make sense of the world and its events: a secure position from which everything may be tested for its bias or sympathy against the certainty of a historical truth.

A friend of mine, Ghaith, who was studying at Cardiff University, once told me how, before the second Intifada, he and his mother and grandfather had sometimes taken the trip from Ramallah to Jaffa to look at their house, which his grandfather had been forced to leave in 1947. One time they knocked at the door, and explained who they were; the Jewish residents reacted coldly. Now I want to ask Ghaith where his grandfather's house is – but then what would I do? Knock on the door myself, and ask to see inside, so I can feel acutely, personally, this outrage on his behalf? What kind of presumptuousness is this fantasy? It is a despicable misery tourism, a melodramatic over-involvement.

In all the cities, Jewish refugees arriving from European detention camps, and survivors of extermination camps – and later, Jews fleeing from the Arab countries, living in the new Israeli state in tent cities – took over empty apartments left by Arab residents who had fled the conflict in 1947 and 1948. Owning nothing, they sometimes kept everything that had belonged to the former inhabitants – the cutlery and crockery, even the framed family photographs. It is both poignant and suspect, that common story, one tragedy erasing or ameliorating or replacing the other. And yet of course, there were ancient and more recent Jewish communities depopulated and destroyed in that war too – in East Jerusalem, and elsewhere.

Walking the streets of Jaffa and Tel Aviv, the evidence is relentless and unavoidable. The duality of the language shimmers, telling one story and erasing another. It lays claim to place in the street names, some of which have imported and imposed European Jewish history and erased the Arab past; it tries to lay claim to what it does not yet own. The naming of the streets in Tel Aviv, this one-hundred-year-old city, everywhere reflects a conscious, deliberate construction: the co-option of the medieval Spanish Hebrew poets, like Ibn Gabirol with his suppurating skin, or the lionisation of Jabotinsky and his expansionist Greater Israel movement – Jabotinsky, whose Jewish Legion formed part of the British army during the First World War, who proposed that an 'iron wall' would be needed to separate Arabs and Jews.

In Holon, near my uncle David's house, there is a cluster of dilapidated buildings on a piece of undeveloped land at the end of Tel Giborim Park, the 'hill of heroes' (every high point, it seems, is a hill of heroes). It is known as the 'Arab village', but my uncle was always evasive and never gave me a clear explanation about it, and now he's dead, and I can't get the story from him at all. I take the bus from Tel Aviv to visit Myriam, his widow, and where the bus stops, at that corner by the 'Arab village', a printed banner is draped over the end wall, declaring 'Na, Nach, Nacham, Nachman me'uman', the religious mantra of the Bratslavers: some of the fervent chanting followers of Rabbi Nachman must be living here. This sign, too, is a claim to what belongs to someone else. And while street names are officially bilingual or trilingual, I notice for the first time now that this is only true on the main roads and the highways. Arabic disappears at the local level. Arabic, in much of Tel Aviv, is virtually invisible. I have never noticed its absence before; now its absence stands exposed like a kind of scar.

On the route between Holon and Tel Aviv, which I travelled countless times as a teenager, the bus passes a Muslim graveyard, marked by its distinctive two-ended graves. Dry, dusty, bounded by the motorway and a highway, it looks like a leftover, abandoned – but it is still in use. All the times that I followed that bus route I never saw it; now I wonder how I could never have seen it. You see what you expect to see; you impose meaning on what you don't understand, and get it wrong, because you draw on the wrong information, because you draw on what you're told you see.

Throughout the city, and throughout the country, someone, or some group, has been spray-painting a blue Star of David on white walls, above the slogan *Am Israel Chai* – 'the nation of Israel lives'. I see it everywhere I go. Sometimes others have amended the Hebrew graffiti delicately. An article on Ynetnews.com gathers images of its variations: in one place it reads 'the nation of Israel lives – by the sword.' In another it is amended to read 'the nation of Israel lives – on American money.' In a third, someone has added an illustration and four letters to the word 'Chai' so that it reads 'the nation of Israel is a snail'.[2] Signs, everywhere, have become signs for something else, signposts to what is not said, to what is concealed, to what is visible but goes unseen. It doesn't require a physical act to render it invisible. A change of language, a change of name, and a continued silence has done a kind of violence to a whole people, and the heroic Hebrew names of Tel Aviv's familiar streets and wide boulevards whisper to me *false, false*, in little sibilant voices.

Eating a shwarma at a window-counter overlooking the intersection of Allenby and Melech King George, trickling tehina over my fingers, watching the street jostle with soldiers and teenagers and middle-aged women in wigs and knee-length skirts, a painful, lonely nostalgia ambushes me. I have loved Israel, and I still love the smell of her, the dust, the sense of wild longing. A secret, shameful part of me still wants to lie down and die in her, but now I am afraid I have lost the right or ability to love even the idea of her. The nostalgia is not only for what I have loved, but for the love itself, infatuated and unambiguous. All this vibrant life, all the argument and provocation of the Israeli Jewish psyche, its in-your-face bluster, its militant, angry, belligerent energy – even if I am losing the ability to love it in simple and absolute ways, because of what it now represents, what it elides or denies, I nevertheless *know* it, I know it in my *kishkes*: it is part of me. How can I excise that? How can I not long for it, and, at the same time, repudiate it?

Along the coast, travelling north from Tel Aviv, everything trembles with this duality – the parched fields, the flocks of goats, ruined houses, new high-rises shimmering in the heat, religious posters plastered on walls and billboards and buses. Always, everywhere, the place-names and road-signs are a cover-up. Over all of it, over its visible existence, there hovers a kind of glamour of another, secret story: not hidden, not quite visible, but implicit. Hard, physical realities, physical facts, they are not quite lies, but they are omissions and half-truths. It is like talking in two languages at once, meanings approaching and approximating each other, sliding in and out of different forms of feeling, of body language and sense. The landscape is alive with a kind of cognitive violence. Though I cannot quite understand what I am seeing, it is impossible not to feel it as a kind of assault.

It's dangerous, this reversal of orientation. Without context you can so easily misconstrue what you're looking at, what you think you might be seeing, and what you're told. Is there any landscape, marked by humans, that isn't made into a geographical palimpsest in this way, layered by waves of conflict and language-change, by migration and settlement? Yet in a landscape that is familiar and loved, one that is navigated by memories and associations and a sharp, poignant sense of affiliation, to become aware of the very different meanings and associations that it might have for other people perhaps does not require any other context.

The bus turns inland at the power station near Hadera, round the bulge of the West Bank towards the Jezreel Valley, where the kibbutz pulls me in. Away from the coastal developments, architecture begins to separate the two communities into Arab town, Jewish town; Arab region, Jewish region. In the city, the boundaries between neighbourhoods, ethnicities and nationalities of origin have blurred and shifted, though socially and politically they still exist, starkly; but once out of the city, the landscape, the architecture, cars, signs, shops all shift back into *Arab, Jewish, Arab, Jewish*. It is not only in the architecture, one with Ottoman references in its minarets, curves, embellishments and colonnades, the other brutalist, modernist, often red-tiled and European; it is also in the way the geography is used. One form of architecture seems built into the land's contours, the other built onto them, but I am seeing what I now expect to see, a new political awareness undermining what I thought I knew, and for the first time making me look for – and romanticise – the evidence of a long connection in that place.

I think the differences are that obvious, and that unmistakable, but of course it is not so simple. Arab town architecture expresses discriminatory planning constraints, not a more organic relationship to the land. Buildings in Arab areas expand outward and upward, storey built on storey to accommodate new generations of a growing family.

As the bus passes through Wadi Ara, I can see the recent changes in the Arab towns: the skeletons of elaborate, prominent new bright villas and houses showing a distinctive inflection of balconies and rooftops and domes, beginning to form whole new neighbourhoods, many built in defiance of planning laws. They differ utterly from the massive white high-rise Jewish neighbourhoods of Herzliya, the tiled structures of the West Bank settlements, and the new pale neighbourhoods of Afula. Afula is transformed. It is no longer the dusty town I knew as a child and teenager by its bus station, a mere transit point: now it also contains within it another past – as Al Fuleh, an Arab village.

Arriving by bus, I find the station itself as I remember it from adolescence, the last time I came by bus to visit the kibbutz. That was twenty-one years ago, for my grand-father's funeral. The station is decrepit and choked with diesel fumes, and the metal benches of the bus bays are crowded with lounging or sleeping soldiers. Raddled, deeply tanned men play chess at the cafe table, and at the entrance to the broken toilets sits the same ancient, silent woman attendant who has been sitting there since the toilets were built. She presides, receiving a shekel for five sheets of toilet paper, like the guardian, the door Porter to the medieval Celtic Otherworld – the one who determines who has earned the right to pass.

Toilets take on a meaning that is almost holy when you're travelling. Your feelings, particularly if you're a woman, are reverent: you approach the promise of a toilet with something like devotion. The women who preside over them, seated at the entrance on a plastic chair, with a little basket for your tribute, speak an ancient pidgin, an archaic Hebrew that is no longer spoken anywhere else. Toilet attendants are indifferent to your needs. You might be at your lowest: your period might have just started, or you may have bled heavily during a long bus-ride and you might be cramped and overfull; you might be suffering from a reaction to the water, or something you ate, incautiously, unwashed – and they observe you, unmoved, unspeaking, waiting for their shekel when you go in, and their tip when you come back out, relieved but vulnerably exposed. They are the embodiment of disinterest, and they make you cringe and scrabble when you are already at your weakest. They see everything and they see right through you; they know you immediately and completely.

The toilet is the only enclosed public space you can enter, in Israel, without being searched, the only public place without a conveyor belt and X-ray machine at the entrance, or a soldier rifling through your papers and dirty underwear, running an explosives detector up and down your body while the impatient queue waits and watches. You retain a kind of public privacy, but that is because they know, those bathroom attendants: they can read you, desperate and reduced to basic need, in an instant. And what is my basic need, now? To know where I belong? To try to do *good* at a time when being Jewish, having a connection to Israel, is seen, increasingly, as something dubious, something that has to be accounted for? Or is the universal estrangement that James Joyce saw in the representative Jew a true estrangement – is exile from yourself a kind of essential Jewish belonging? Perhaps my alienation, at forty, at last has made me into this real kind of Jew. I wonder if these are our only choices – to carry our homeland in a book; to carry our homeland in our heart; to carry no homeland at all. But the toilet attendant in the Afula bus station is not the Oracle at Delphi. Impassive, unmoved, she accepts my tribute. She's seen it all before; she's seen every species of need and abasement. Impassive, unmoved, she watches me move out again into the noise of the world, lost and confused and full of longing.

My mother's brother Asaf meets me outside the bus station, and drives me to the kibbutz. He laughs at my eulogy of the toilet attendant, my nostalgia for the Israel of my childhood when nothing worked and everyone was poor, when Jews were good and Arabs were dangerous and I didn't doubt anything. We turn onto the Ruler Road and drive past the fishponds, now obscured by tall rushes, past a spur-winged plover bobbing at the edge of the dusty tarmac, past the familiar prison, unchanged. Ahead of us the green trilingual road sign points left for Kibbutz Beit Hashita, straight on for the town of Beit She'an, and Asaf begins to slow for the turning. Over the years I have picked up a few Arabic swearwords and exclamations, but it is only recently that I have learned to read the alphabet. Slowly, the meaning of the road sign emerges for the first time: the word in Arabic does not spell *Beisan*, the Arabic name for the town that lies straight on, near the border with Jordan, but *Beit She'an*, its Hebrew name. I notice the same thing, later, on the way to Jerusalem: the Arabic on the road sign does not give *Al Quds*, but the Hebrew name for Jerusalem, *Yerushala'im*.

Asaf parks near his small house. Outside the cool of the air-conditioned car the dry heat catches at me. Fallen eucalyptus blades crackle under my feet, and their scent rises – and with the scent the place closes its fist over my heart. The memory of every return wakes, every childhood and adolescent and adult return – the memory of riding on the back of my grandfather's small tractor, and he turning his head to smile at me that warm wordless expression of affection; my mother, vibrant and glowing; walking hand-in-hand with my older sister, and the revelation of the birds, one after another, *sunbird, hoopoe, roller, bee-eater, palm dove, bulbul* – smaller and brighter than in the field-guide, and though new, known instantly, sharp and exciting...

But my mother is distant and my grandfather is dead. My sister is dead, too, and many of the birds of our shared childhood have disappeared as well, gone long ago: the Egyptian vultures, gone from the edges of the roads, along with the rubbish and carrion, and gone, like the black kites, from the great dump near Tel Aviv, which is now covered over and landscaped, like the coal-tips in south Wales. My innocence is gone, too: that municipal dump, once a bird-haven, and for me a bird excitement, also seals in the invisible remnants of a depopulated and destroyed Arab village called Al-Khayriyya.

Over lunch, Asaf asks what exactly it is I'm after, and so, rather nervously, I tell him how I found out about the villages of Al Murassas and Yubla from my mother, and how I want to know what happened in this place before 1948. I'm not sure how he'll respond. Perhaps he'll see it as an unwelcome digging up of what is better left alone, but he doesn't. 'Wallah!' he exclaims with enthusiasm. 'This is so interesting.' We can check in the kibbutz archive, he tells me, and he knows where the site of Al Murassas is: he can take me there, though there's not much to see.

I feel a jiggle of excitement, the beginnings of a kind of hope crystallising in me – of revelation or epiphany, an anticipation of some kind of confrontation with the harsh fact of destruction. I wonder if it will *move* me, if it will shift me from my ambivalent uncertainties and confusions. My confusion has increased – I am in the grip of nostalgia, and during the night I cannot sleep: all my senses are in full assault, flooded by the sound, the smell, the familiar layout of this place that was my mother's place, this place where, somehow, I became aware of myself as a separate creature for the first time.

But when my uncle takes me to Al Murassas the next day, it's a disappointment. We drive along a pale dusty road that meanders through treeless slopes of unfenced crop-fields, and he slows and then stops the car near a small stand of trees, where a barbed-wire fence encloses a rough area of dry cow pasture and sabra. The fawn-coloured cows are slow with the heat, and turn sleepily to look at us.

'Here you are,' he says, gesturing at the cows.

'Where are we?' I ask.

'This is it,' he says. 'This is Al Murassas.' He points out

the wildly growing prickly pear, which shows the presence of a former settlement. Originally it was planted to define boundaries between households; now it is a thicket. He thinks that someone important is buried near the trees, that the trees mark the location of a grave. 'Yubla has nothing left,' he says. 'Even less than Al Murassas. There's nothing to see, nothing to mark the site, but we can go if you want.'

All I can see is the cattle and the wild thicket of old cactus. Al Murassas is just dust and stones and cows, a few trees, sabra. I know what I was expecting, what I was hoping for – something tragic; an epiphany. Instead I am merely hot, and tired. I look out over ruin with half my attention and feel only a pressure on my bladder, the awkwardness of intruding, suspect, on someone else's past, and the rapid anticlimax of my unfulfilled desire to be changed utterly. The nagging readjustment turns into irritation. I shake my head, and say there is no need to go and see where Yubla used to be.

In the kibbutz archive, Tomer, the archivist, remembers Al Murassas and Yubla. She doesn't know when precisely in 1948 they were destroyed, and doesn't say who actually carried out the destruction. 'This was political – it came from the government,' she says. 'It was not the decision of the kibbutz to destroy the villages.' Like my mother, she remembers walking in Al Murassas when the buildings were still standing, some months after the inhabitants had left. She thinks the villagers of Al Murassas and Yubla were neither Bedouin nor Arab, but a different ethnic group. She remembers them as being very dark; she thinks perhaps they were African – perhaps descended from some of the African people who were brought to Palestine as slaves and servants in the earlier Ottoman period.

The houses of Al Murassas and Yubla were built of adobe. They only stayed empty and intact for a short while before they were destroyed. When Tomer was a child, nothing was safe. There was a high protective fence around the kibbutz, and people stood guard at night on the roofs of the school and the children's house. By day things were amicable; at night there were attacks. They had lived daily in a state of threat from their neighbours in all the years leading up to the War of Independence in 1948. Afterwards, it was safer. Afterwards, the land left by the fleeing Arab villagers was shared out for use by the neighbouring kibbutzim.

Tomer, my mother, and others their age: all of them remember the ruins of Yubla, and Al Murassas. What happened to the villages is in the memory of the earlier generation, too – in their *yiskor* books, memorial pamphlets published for each member after his or her death, and kept there in the archive. Everyone of my mother's generation remembers a version of Yubla and Al Murassas. They know, but don't know; they know but they don't talk about it, or they skate over it. Like my mother, most don't want to be reminded, don't want to dwell on the implications of that knowledge, or those memories. It is one thing to oppose the separation wall, to disclaim East Jerusalem, to argue for a full pull-out of the West Bank, but it is quite another to talk about the right of return of those refugees, now in their millions, who fled or were expelled between 1947 and 1949, some of whom were expelled a second time in 1967.

The older generation, and my mother's generation, remember. They remember the field boundaries and know the location of the destroyed village sites. But members of the younger generation never knew and have not been told,

and but for the efforts of individual historians and organisations like Zochrot dedicated to memorialising the Nakba,
that knowledge would be gone from national memory too,
as the names are gone from the maps.

Maps of this place used to be simple and sparse, like all
early maps – but now they're complex and crowded, dense
and layered. Embedded in the Western imagination, the
place has been redrawn by explorers and holy men, by
missionaries and emissaries of Empire, and by Empire
itself, its surface imagined and recreated, or observed and
recorded, and its names and meanings mapped onto space
sacred to other people, too – the Welsh, for example, and the
white colonisers of America. The old Western maps
combine the present and the past, juxtaposing what can be
observed with what is imagined. On nineteenth-century
and early twentieth-century maps, biblical Hebrew place-
names in pretty Gothic font lie alongside Arabic names and
the modern Hebrew names in Roman font, and there are
the modern Hebrew names of the new Jewish towns of
Gadera or Tel Aviv. Later, the new Jewish settlements are
added: the kibbutzim, and communal farms, and villages.
And then in 1955 the map reaches what is perhaps the peak
of its complexity, with the triumphant purple overprint of
the word *harus* – destroyed. After that, the Israeli maps
revert to a simpler form, and the tourist maps for long years
have not even shown what is known in Hebrew as 'the
seam', the physically erased border with the West Bank. All
of it became seamlessly Israel.

Israel's enemies say it should be wiped off the map,
meaning it should be utterly destroyed and its name obliterated. That is what Israel has done to the Palestinian
villages. But in wiping the village sites and the record of
their destruction off the map, it has obliterated its own past,

too: the history of its birth, and the history of the years before its birth.

Beit Hashita is on every map of Israel, but the Arab villages are gone, as their physical features are gone from the landscape. And yet, though they're gone, their memory is not obliterated in that place, not entirely, not yet. There's nothing to see of Al Murassas but sabra and stones and sleepy cows, but there are unmarked graves there. Someone's grandparents and great-grandparents are buried there, as they are in Yubla and Kafra, in Wadi El Bireh, Al Hamidiya, Jabbul and Kawkab al Hawa and all the other destroyed villages and neighbourhoods – as mine are buried, just a few kilometres away. But my ancestors' graves are marked and maintained, and they have gathered a scatter of small stones, each of which records a visit, a paying of respects.

You consult a map to find out where you are, to see how to get from there to where you wish to be. This is how you *orientate* yourself, situating yourself, according to the meaning of the word, in relation to the rising sun, but also in relation to Jerusalem, as churches are aligned to point east to their origins. Jerusalem, and the whole land for which it is a synecdoche, forms the linguistic foundation of how, in English, you articulate knowing where you are.

But I don't know where I am. No map I consult can tell me. I have no idea where I am in relation to my personal orient. The whole landscape, physical and imagined, shimmers with duality, with signs and stories that *dis*-orientate. Perhaps I will always be disorientated, because there is no longer any absolute east. It depends on where you are. Perhaps, like my mother, I may only carry my homeland in my heart, in a longing that will not be appeased, that cannot really be appeased, because others with grandparents buried in this place also carry their homeland in their hearts this way. But I am permitted to return, to leave a stone as a mark of my visit, to pay my respects and feel, here, my roots – and they are not.

# 3 – Love and longing

I knew at ten who was an Arab and who was not an Arab. No one told me: I just knew. The division wasn't one of Arab and Jew; it was Arabs and everyone else. Arabs were dangerous, and at the same time primitive and contemptible; 'Arabs', and all that 'they' constituted, were always understood in their generality, reduced and impersonal. I knew what Arabs were like from my grandfather's wound, an emblem of their violent dangerousness. I knew who was an Arab when my father's hand tightened around mine in the central bus station, or in the street; I knew it when a young man in discoloured Y-fronts had tried to touch me sexually at the Sakhne, a hot-water spring at the foot of Gilboa, because he slipped into the water from the far shore, the Arab side, where we didn't go, where men stood too close together and dropped rubbish, and made noise. It was not articulated, but it was understood. As a child I could not have recognised this as an implacable biological reduction of others to something less than human. Now, as an adult, when I encounter it in others, when I am confronted by it in members of my family, I can only reluctantly acknowledge having thought it or felt it myself, because my whole story, my whole sense of self has been premised on reducing the humanity of Arabs in general and any Arab as an individual. A clear sense of 'them' – sly, unclean, mendacious and sexually intemperate – has helped to safeguard my understanding of 'us' collectively, each encircling ring of 'us': family, kibbutz, nation-state – and its necessity.

But when, after visiting the archive, my uncle Asaf takes me to see Abu Omar, I fall in love. Abu Omar is the grandfather of a woman who used to work at the kibbutz factory. According to Asaf he is old, and remembers everything. He lives in the village of Na'ura, which lies some ten kilometres from the kibbutz. Although most Arab villages in the valley were depopulated in 1948 and later destroyed, Na'ura is one of a group whose inhabitants remained. They left for a short while early in 1948, and then returned. Unlike many other Arab citizens of Israel, who became 'internal refugees' – the 'present absent', as they are known in Hebrew – villagers of Na'ura and a handful of other Arab settlements in the western end of the valley were allowed by Jewish militia to come back. But the story of what had happened in these villages is contested. One version is that rather than being driven out by Jewish soldiers, the villagers were instead ordered by Arab army irregulars to evacuate, apparently because of a fear that they would come to some 'understanding' with Jewish forces, which, it seemed, they did – in this version, they were, in short, 'collaborators'.

On the phone to Abu Omar, Asaf explains briefly that I want to know about 'how things had been before 1948'. I can hear a man talking loudly, asking questions, and then stating something, emphatic. Hanging up, Asaf says, 'OK, we'll go tomorrow afternoon. But,' he adds, and he smiles slightly, 'don't eat too much beforehand, because they'll feed us.' He pauses. 'It will be a *lot* of food... You should leave some room.'

The next day my uncle and I drive down to highway 71, and then turn off through the hills to Na'ura. Children and women watch us curiously as we creep up through the winding village, past the mosque with its green glass. At the top of the village, Asaf parks in the shade by an open shed where a sorrel mare tosses her head irritably at the flies. A barn full of hay holds chickens and a few penned sheep. I have only stopped in an Arab village once before to visit people, and the unfamiliarity makes me feel like a voyeur. Apart from neighbours of a childhood friend in the Galilee back in the late 1980s and again in 2007, I have never met and socialised with any Arab people in Israel. I don't want to admit this; it contorts me with embarrassment that it's true.

Abu Omar is sitting outside at a picnic table. Chickens are stepping and pecking in the dust and dry grass around the legs of the white plastic chairs, and a man with intense blue eyes is arguing with him, leaning forward, his elbow on the table. He's a kibbutznik from Tel Yosef, and a teacher in the nearby secondary school. His manner is at the same time both deferential and emphatic.

Abu Omar greets my uncle and nods at me. Then he leans back in his chair and, without turning, shouts towards the open doorway of the house behind him. Out of sight, an older woman answers, and a little later a young woman comes out with a tray of drinks. She ducks her head and smiles at us shyly as we each take a glass. We wait, drinking sweet, ice-cold lemonade and batting away the flies, while Abu Omar and the teacher finish making their arrangements. The teacher has asked Abu Omar to come and talk to his class about how things used to be before the 1948 war for Israeli independence. 'But listen,' he says, smiling, as he gets up to leave, 'remember – don't make the Jews look too good.'

Abu Omar shrugs. '*Beseder*,' he says. 'OK,' and he turns to us. We go into the house, into a living room hung with framed images – a white stallion, colour-saturated photographic portraits of young men, a shiny gold and blue rendition of the Dome of the Rock. Abu Omar sits on a couch and talks to my uncle. He doesn't look at me as my uncle explains what I am interested in hearing.

I am fixed on his heavy jowled face, its dark clusters of moles and melanin marks. He wears a crisp white keffiyeh, and a faded suit jacket over his dishdasha. He is eighty, but his voice, when he begins his account of the past, is liquid and sing-song. It is a storyteller's delivery; what he tells he's told many times before. My uncle sits beside me, transfixed, but with my flattened, standardised, unidiomatic learner's Hebrew, clumsy from disuse, I find it hard to understand. Abu Omar's Hebrew is richly idiomatic and embellished, and his accent strong and unfamiliar.

Soon we are interrupted. Young men begin to drift into the house one by one. They stand against the wall, or crouch, waiting. Abu Omar looks through a capacious battered leather satchel that lies beside him on the couch, and pulls out packets of envelopes, strapped in large rubber bands. He leafs through these, and then, finding the right packet, removes the rubber band and hands over a sheaf of envelopes to the man who is crouching nearby. There is little talk. Then, when the young man has looked all the way through the sheaf he's been given, he nods and says something and rises and leaves, and another takes his place.

My uncle leans towards me. 'Abu Omar is the postman,' he explains. 'The trouble is, everyone is called Zoabi, so he has to know – he *does* know – everyone, everything.' The naming convention always amuses my uncle. He's explained to me before that Na'ura is a village of the Zoabi clan. I think of the common names of Wales – Jones, Williams, Hughes, Morgan – and the ways in which individuals are distinguished from one another by place of birth or residence: John Jones Y Bala, Dai Jones Tregaron, and, more locally, by farm or house name – Jane Morgan

Aberdauddwr. That too causes amusement to outsiders. It is surely similar here. Not so far back my own family had Goldsteins on one side, Gelsteins on the other, like a Jewish joke. A diversity of names indicates a diversity of origins, I think, and a network of shared names is the signpost to a rootedness in one place – or, in the Jewish case, rootedness in one people. But of course Goldstein and Gelstein are invented names, replacements: further back, people were identified by their parents, by place, by their husbands. Surnames are a recent innovation, but clan names are not.

It is late afternoon, and the men are stopping by after they've finished work to collect the post for their families. Abu Omar's oldest son comes in and sits quietly. He talks a little with some of the men who are waiting, and to my uncle. Then, as the last of the other men are leaving, Abu Omar's grandson comes in. He shakes hands with my uncle and nods to me and sits down in a chair nearby. Abu Omar explains to him who I am, reminds him who Asaf is. He smiles at me and says 'Welcome' in English. But I am not paying attention to anything that's being said as we are introduced, and later, afterwards, I cannot remember his name, and cannot ask: when I mention him, my uncle and aunt look at me, suspicious; the interest in my voice betrays me.

I am stricken the moment I see him. He is beautiful. He's a little heavy-set, his hair very short, so short it makes him look somehow vulnerable around the ears and temples, and this arouses in me a sharp tenderness. *Coup de foudre* – it's only happened to me once before, like this, like a blow. He is so beautiful I think I might not ever recover from it.

When the two women bring food to the living room door, a tray with bowls of *ful* in sauce, with rice, lamb, pita, and cucumber and yoghurt, he gets up and takes it from them, and puts it down on a low table in front of me and Asaf.

Abu Omar pulls over a chair. He gestures to me to eat, but I don't know how to proceed. I apologise that I don't know the etiquette, and his grandson smiles at my discomfiture.

He has dimples.

'There are no rules,' he says. 'You're not going to offend anyone. Eat and enjoy. You won't have food like this again.'

He doesn't eat – he says he has already eaten. 'There is no food like food from home,' he says. 'I've travelled, but I have never had food as good as the food here.' His Hebrew is quite unlike his grandfather's. His accent is that of a first-language speaker, and he is fluently bilingual. 'When my grandfather talks, I always come and listen, because I always learn something new,' he says.

There is something very still and collected about him, and he is so beautiful that I lose my appetite. I am afraid to make a mistake, afraid that I will eat clumsily. The lamb is tender, without any fat, and when I smile at him, I realise too late that shreds of meat are caught in my teeth. My heart starts to race with embarrassment; overheated, I can feel sweat gathering and beginning to trickle between my breasts. Physically full of discomfort, betrayed by my body – how inconveniently love or desire makes you victim of your body's fluids.

Abu Omar asks my uncle, 'Does she have a family? Is she married?'

'Yes, she has a family,' Asaf replies.

I want to correct him; I want to interject and say, 'No, no – tell him I have two nearly grown-up daughters, and that I'm divorced.'

Earlier Abu Omar said, 'We are all people of the Book. It's only forbidden for Muslims to marry someone without a genuine faith, without a book.' According to him, if a Jewish woman read the Qu'ran it would be enough – she would not have to convert; that was between her and God. Faith was an individual, private matter. 'People without a real religion, a religion without a book – now that is a problem,' he said.

'What about the Druze?' I asked.

Even the Druze were forbidden to Muslims, according to Abu Omar, because their religion was a secret faith – there was no holy text.

'Tell him I've read the Qu'ran,' I want to say to Asaf now, but instead I smile carefully, not showing my teeth, and nod and say nothing.

Abu Omar tells stories about a stolen tractor, about the British, about a donkey he had once owned that was shot. He was sixteen then, in 1948, and remembers it, but his stories are almost rote. He is not speaking with the live hesitations of remembering, but with the easy flow of recitation. The stories have clearly been told many times. Like any practised story teller, he wants to be the one to choose his material, and not be distracted from the narrative he's following. It is awkward to interfere with that flow, and it is difficult to ask questions: with my limited vocabulary, I struggle to understand his colloquial Arabic Hebrew, and he doesn't seem to understand me, and only with reluctance and quite evident discomfort addresses me directly if I speak. So I speak through my uncle. I ask why people left in 1948.

'It was Qawuqji – it was Qawuqji and his men, making trouble, making people afraid. They were afraid! So they left,' he says. He asks Asaf if I know who Qawuqji was – and so I answer Asaf when he turns to me, in a way that is becoming comical. Fawzi Qawuqji had been the commander of the Arab Liberation Army; he'd led Iraqi forces from Jordan. It is more or less right.

'And why did some people here not leave, then?' I ask.

Again Abu Omar looks at my uncle, not at me, when he answers. 'We weren't afraid. We knew it would be OK.' He gives a complicated account of who had spoken to whom. They had received assurances from the kibbutzniks. 'We had a good relationship,' he says. He mentions Yosef Dagan, 'the Jewish mukhtar', as they had called him, a member of the kibbutz who had negotiated the land purchases.

It is clumsy of me to ask whether people ever came back at all to visit, and whether he has any contact now, or had in the past, with those who left. Only afterwards I realise how this question must have sounded. Under the circumstances, despite my uncle's solid validating presence and credentials, my own background is completely unknown. For whom might I be gathering information? 'No,' Abu Omar says shortly. 'No' – and clearly that is a story he does not wish to tell. 'Look,' he explains, 'I am an Israeli. Things are good. We are all right. Everything is all right. For this, some people would call me a traitor.' He laughs. 'But as far as the refugees are concerned, it's difficult. For a lot of people, why would they come back? They have jobs, and houses – in Amman, in Beirut, in Europe. Why would they want to come back? What would they have here? But the people in camps – they have nothing. For them, it's different. For them...'

What the teacher from Tel Yosef meant when he said 'don't make the Jews look too good,' begins to make sense. In 1948 the Zoabi clan had stayed, several villages of the clan, and their relationship with the kibbutzim is good. Abu Omar's view of the past, and of present relations, is one of accommodation and co-existence – or at least publicly it is. But that isn't true for a younger generation of Arab Israelis, or Palestinian citizens of Israel. Hanin Zoabi, a Knesset Member, is more outspoken, for which, targeted by the right wing, she has been repeatedly censured, and suspended from the Knesset. For her, this old man and his desire for accommodation would no doubt embody the 'good Arab' which, in her political position, she repudiates. I wonder how things look to Abu Omar's grandson, but with Abu Omar there it is impossible to ask him if he sees things the same way as his grandfather. How does the past look to his cousin who, before she married, had worked for my uncle as a business manager and bookkeeper in the kibbutz factory? How can I ask, how can I press any point, ask difficult questions, when we are there as guests, when the relationship between kibbutz and village, between families, is amicable? I don't want to make trouble; I don't want to disturb that relationship. If I were alone, perhaps I could ask about those who see things differently, could probe that question of accommodation, which some see as treachery and collaboration. But if I were alone I would not be talking to Abu Omar.

After the meal we have pastries, and sweet tea made from camomile and sage. Abu Omar collects the herbs every day on the hills. There are pans of flowers drying in the hallway where the two women sit talking and eating. The women have not been introduced. One of them is Abu Omar's very young second wife, Asaf tells me later; he thinks perhaps the other woman is a daughter-in-law.

When we are leaving, Abu Omar says he'll give me some of his dried tea mixture, but his grandson says, 'No, you can't do that! You'll give her so much trouble when she gets to Britain – what will they think it is?' He smiles at me, showing his dimples.


Later on, afterwards, I can't remember anything much else about Abu Omar's grandson – not his walk, his name. All I remember is that dimpled smile, and his kind, amused brown eyes. But he haunts me. Everywhere I go his beautiful face returns and expands, diffused into every Arab man I see. Back in Tel Aviv I watch each man who passes with an assessing, sexually predatory eye. Walking south to Jaffa, the look is returned, because I am looking. I am forty and unattached, my daughters nearly grown, the tug of duty and responsibility beginning to weaken, a heavy grief cutting loose – and some kind of adolescent lonely longing is alive in me again. I am in the grip of desire without object. I *want*... I don't know what I want. Risk, fear, adventure: to feel the agitated pulse of my life.

The Israeli soldier was my fetish once. For his qualities, to which I signed up in my early teens – silent and suffering, wounded and heroic, dusty, army-booted, emotional but tough – I felt, always, an erotic, dark tenderness. I've lost that now. Israelis used to travel the year after they finished the army: they'd go to India or Latin America, get stoned for a while, and then go back to do *milu'im*, their few weeks' annual army service. It has changed since then, since my adolescence. Doing military service in the Occupied Territories exacts a different sort of price; the soldiers of the protest groups Yesh Gvul and Breaking the Silence testify to it. Israelis still leave, afterwards, but those I knew when I lived in the US weren't going to go back. They'd outstayed their visas and formally disappeared, working illegally on building sites and in restaurant kitchens. They were vulnerable, trying to erase a past; they were without a future, without a clear identity. It was a different kind of wound. I remember Nadav, who played the sitar and smoked too much weed – how could I fetishise gentle Nadav with his peering short-sightedness, his fine musician's fingers, his gentleness and sensitivity?

The ache of desire is *sehnsucht, hiraeth, saudade* – a tearing loneliness of the soul, a longing to come home. Instead of carrying my homeland in a book, in my heart, it has transferred to beautiful men with luminous dark eyes – 'the enemy', 'the other', since I can no longer love my own. And by this reduction of each individual man to a representative, and by my expansion of each exchange, real or fantasy, into a universal exchange between me, Jew, and him, Arab, I know I am committing in my fevered imagination every sin of exotification and objectification, of orientalism and sexual imperialism. The critic, the academic in me watches how I reduce 'the Arab' to an object of desire – and at the same time I cannot stop myself from looking and desiring. How we neglect women as imperial savages, as though, being ourselves disenfranchised, or victims of men's desires, we cannot ourselves be victimisers, colonisers – as though we cannot ourselves make others into some kind of object. And of course it's only Arab *men* I am looking at this way, because women return me to myself, and I don't want to look at myself. I want to be wanted, not challenged. I want to be sought after, desired. I want to say *yes* to everything, to follow every path that opens up before me, to feel alive, connected.

'Fetishising the enemy,' my cousin says to me later over garish red cocktails we're drinking at an outside bar on Dizengoff Street, in Tel Aviv. 'Jewish self-hatred. That's what the right wing think all left-wing critics of Zionism are guilty of.' He makes a face when he tastes his drink. 'I just don't seem to like alcohol,' he says, disappointed.

Jewish self-hatred? I know what people mean by it, but it's not true of me. According to that view, any criticism of Israel is a criticism of your Jewish self, shows a disconnection and corruption in your Jewish core, and yet it is because I cannot hate my Jewishness, and cannot hate Israel that I feel conflicted. They are right, however, about my other guilt – fetishising Arabs.

Now, wandering the streets of Jaffa, of Tel Aviv, in Ramallah and Jerusalem, I am obsessed with Arabs, with Arab men, with one Arab man I see in all Arab men – nameless, beautiful, forbidden: a fetish.

That shift from fear to desire does not happen because my childhood apprehension has been overcome. Of course what you fear can be erotic, too; fear also fuels desire. That apprehension, in every sense of the word – a notion, an idea; a comprehension or understanding; an anxious antic- ipation, fear or dread – skulks powerful and threatening in my subconscious, barely contained by my conscientiously liberal worldview. I am afraid of Arabs – an idea of Arabs in their generality, and individual Arabs in their particularity. It is something I learned deeply as a child; it was a founda- tional principle, a fundamental of my part in the collective that was *not* that, *not* Arab.


My aunt Myriam is afraid. Since the death of my uncle David things have been very difficult for her. Alone in the tiny house they built in Holon, a town that has become a suburb of Tel Aviv, the huge flat-screen television which is never turned off shows her twenty-four-hour news of threat and violence and war. My cousins and their young children are in financial difficulties, and so is she. She used to travel, but since she broke her back, falling in Portugal, she has not gone anywhere. Her back has healed, but now she feels more vulnerable than ever.

Myriam is the same age as Abu Omar. Her family emigrated from Morocco to Israel not in the panicked

Jewish exodus from Arab states after Israeli independence, but later, in the early sixties. She'd gone to Paris first; she has always been very much orientated towards France, where one of her sisters lives. Her parents had been observant and strict. When I went to visit them for a Shabbat meal as a teenager, I was confused by the constraints, by the silent, Shabbat-barricaded streets in their religious neighbourhood in the coastal town of Netanya.

Myriam is tiny. She has shrunk from osteoporosis and arthritis, but she looks after her appearance carefully. Her dark brown hair is thick and curly, and she dresses with style, in exquisite hand-printed fabrics. And she is warm, expressive, fiercely devoted to family. Even though she is uneasy about my politics, my questions, my friendship with Palestinians, she makes me welcome. She always makes me welcome.

My uncle David had been afraid, too. He had travelled a great deal – to Nepal, Ethiopia, Eritrea, Vietnam, as a consultant specialist in insect control in grain storage. When he visited us in England during my childhood, he used to bring exotic conditions – dysentery, malaria – and beautiful gifts: bracelets from India, carvings from east Africa. He had a Monty Python humour, a crude schoolboy repartee. David was politically and socially liberal in most areas except where Arabs were concerned. With 'the Arabs', gradually, he had given up, and late in his life, ill and in pain, he began to indulge his fear, his credulity, and his wife's deeply-held prejudices. Their tiny house was fitted with burglar alarms and motion sensors. The sliding door into the back yard was secured with a metal shutter. The front windows were protected by heavy metal grilles.

In the summer of 2007, when I visited with my younger daughter, David was already very ill, and vulnerable. He described the shoddy work on the house done by Arab builders – how the workers had stolen building materials; how they had deliberately mis-measured a doorway, so that the door didn't fit; how they had laid floor tiles incorrectly, so that they were coming loose. Never again, he and Myriam said: now they'd not hire Arab workers. Their neighbours had been broken into. They said that Palestinians came from the Territories and stole – cars, mostly, as well as taking anything to hand, but they organised targeted thefts, too, of expensive items, specialised technology: robbery to order, a kind of criminal commissioning.

My daughter and I were heading to Ramallah to visit Ghaith, my friend who was a student at Cardiff University, and David didn't think we should go. It wasn't safe, he said. He was concerned about physical danger, but also concerned that I might be used.

'Used *how*?' I asked.

'How well do you know these people?' he said.

'Well enough,' I said, 'to trust them.'

My unvoiced outrage did not entirely displace a niggling moment of doubt – was I being naive? I thought of Ghaith, of his mass of curly black hair, his piercings, his splay-footed walk, and it was laughable to doubt. Nevertheless, it did not seem a good idea to mention that his parents had been members of the Popular Front for the Liberation of Palestine. I didn't in fact know them at all.

'Why should you go there?' Myriam said. 'Can't your friend come here?'

'It's hard for him to get a permit: he's the wrong age,' I told her.

'Good, I'm glad,' she said. 'Why should they come here? If they want to go somewhere they can go to Jordan, to Saudi…'

My aunt had welcomed me; she had embraced my daughter. She had said, 'This is your home: please feel completely at home.' I was her guest. I could not engage with the enormity of what she'd just said. When she made such a pronouncement, as her guest I could not say anything that was in my mind. To have said it would have been an abuse of hospitality, and for my Moroccan aunt, hospitality was close to something sacred.

Instead I picked up plates and bowls and took them outside to the table in the back yard where we would eat. We were getting ready for a family gathering – one of my cousins was coming over with his wife and children to see us. The adobe walls of the house and yard were painted an orange ochre, and the shutters and gate and woodwork were cobalt blue. All the woodwork had been made by my uncle years before: outside, the window frames and shutters and fence; inside, the furniture and the stairs and banisters, and, hanging on the walls, some of the ouds and guitars he'd made before he'd cut off the top joint of his thumb with a saw. He'd put his piece of thumb in a bag of ice and driven to hospital, but the doctors had been unable to reattach it.

My uncle lifted the edge of the tablecloth. 'Look,' he said, bending over and showing me the hole in the end of the hollow frame of the metal trestle-table. There in the opening floated a tiny face of poison and danger, black-patterned, with yellow antennae. Another appeared behind it, jostling to come out, and delicately, lightly, the first one climbed to the edge and floated off towards me, trailing long, finely jointed black and yellow legs. I backed away from it. Those wasp colours of alarm and patterns of attack were my deepest childhood fear, fear on an irrational scale – a phobia.

Around my bare legs another had arrived, waiting, float-ing, wanting to go in. There was a little crust of mud in the entryway. 'They're building a nest there,' my uncle said, smiling at them. 'They're mud wasps. Aren't they wonder-ful?' Seeing my reaction, he tried to reassure me. 'They're not like the *common* wasp,' he said. 'I don't think they even sting,' but to me that didn't matter – the colour scheme, and that arbitrary movement, whose meaning I could not inter-pret as anything but threat, meant only imminent attack.

Knowing so deep inside you danger, violent danger, can you react as if it were otherwise? Can you ever undo the way the angry face, those terrible mandibles and that bisected abdomen, those violently contrasting colours, have burned into you the knowledge – often mistaken, but knowledge nevertheless – of *attack*? Perhaps you can change it, if you want to: you can study the habits, the meanings of its movements; you can watch it build its complicated nest, and observe its delicate communications. Gradually increasing exposure is one method for trying to overcome a phobia. But I didn't want to understand, and in some fundamental way I did not want to lose my fear, either, to feel better about wasps, because what I felt was also a kind of hatred: when I saw a wasp, what I wanted unequivocally was for it to die. Even when I had killed them *en masse* with ant-powder in a ground nest near my house, and had come the next day to find the dead heaped in the entryway – piles of bodies, multiples, a horror of waspness – it had made little difference that they were dead. In stasis they still carried with them the reminder of that insistent weaving attack movement, and I wanted them not so much dead, as never to have existed.

Despite the doubts my uncle had voiced, I went with my daughter to Ramallah anyway, on the way south to Eilat, smug in my own liberalism, repudiating what I dismissed as his ignorant mistrust, my aunt's prejudice and fear, and it started to go wrong before we even left Holon. My phone ran out of credit and I could not find any way to top it up: it was Shabbat and everything was shut. I had told Ghaith approximately what time we'd get to the Qalandia check-point, where he'd meet us at the other side, but we got there earlier than I'd estimated, and I could not contact him to say we'd arrived.

This was 2007, the first occasion in years that I had spent any extended time in Israel, apart from a week's visit to family the previous year, and this was the first time I was visiting the West Bank since before the start of the Intifada in 1987. Though I had seen the high, heavy separation fence from the top of Mount Gilboa, the approach to Qalandia gave me my first sight of the notorious wall section of the barrier. It had settled into the land, concrete and cement weathering quickly in the heat. The checkpoint was in a barren landscape of waste ground, with rubbish caught in the low scrub. I felt it ought to have been somehow momentous, the first time passing through, as though we'd entered a war zone, but the brutality of the wall and its watchtowers had, through over-exposure to its image, become normalised and unremarkable. It was only remarkable in its ordinariness.

There was no other traffic going through, and we were waved straight on without being stopped. The Qalandia checkpoint was frequently violent, and it was the one place I did not want to wait. Ours was the only car in the wide empty lot on the far side of the barrier. Though there was little traffic coming from the Israeli side, there were plenty of people trying to cross the other way. Heavy traffic crawled on the road towards and past the checkpoint in a blare of horns. A military jeep sped by, blue lights flashing.

Sitting alone and conspicuous in the empty car park, waiting for Ghaith to arrive, we were soon enough targeted by a ragged streetseller, who leaned towards the window, gesturing to me to open it. He held up bags of spices – green *za'tar*, and powdered red sumac – and knocked on the window. British politeness, fear of causing offence, made me open it, and he thrust a bag of sumac at me. 'Only ten shekels,' he said.

When I refused, and began closing the window, he asked, 'How much you pay?' and when I shook my head he began to get angry. 'Take it, take it, I give it to you,' he said, and he reached through the window and put the bag of sumac in my lap. I handed it back, closed the window and looked away, kicking myself, frightened. Not three minutes across the border and I had been a foolish tourist, and now an angry streetseller was shambling off to – to *what*, exactly? I told myself the fears were absurd, but they had proliferated and grown ugly by the time Ghaith stepped out of a taxi in front of us.

The centre of Ramallah was the way I remembered much of Israel as a child – full of diesel fumes and ruinous buses, crowded and noisy. But in the stillness of the middle-class residential neighbourhoods, with their rose gardens and pale stone houses, Israel seemed a long way away – until we walked to the Quaker school, and looked out over the valley at the mass of white Jewish settlement buildings clustered on the crest of the hill opposite. After lunch in a quiet shaded restaurant, Ghaith refused to let me pay, or contribute. 'You're my guests,' he said.

Getting through the checkpoint late that afternoon was more complicated than coming the other way. We inched forward in a crush of cars, all trying to cut across one another. Boys squeezed sideways between wing mirrors, knocking on car windows and gesturing with their goods – packs of cigarettes and bags of sumac, kites in the shape of military jets. I couldn't make out the frequent loudspeaker announcements from the soldiers' booths. In Ramallah itself I had not felt afraid, but at the Qalandia checkpoint the atmosphere was tense and angry.

My anxiety increased as we were searched and questioned: the pressure to get out was building behind me, and building in me, reinforced by the watchtowers, the booths, the heavy, ominous mass of the wall. Now its concrete physicality and power became real and felt, as we were suspended, exposed, caught on the cusp between inside and outside, waiting to be allowed to exit, or enter.

When, at last, we were waved through, I drove off in the wrong direction, and with my attention not fully on the road I hit the curb hard, and shortly after felt with sickening certainty the lopsided sagging crunch of a punctured tyre. We were out of sight of the checkpoint, round the bend from it, and there was nothing but the great blind expanse of the wall on one side, and waste ground on the other. I had no way to make a phone-call and we had to walk back to the checkpoint to ask a soldier if I could borrow a phone.

The soldiers laughed among themselves, gesturing towards us with their chins. One of the bus drivers came over and pointed out a man who, he said, would be happy to change the tyre. The man was tall and silent. He walked back with us and got to work without saying a word. By the time he had finished changing the tyre it was getting dark. He wouldn't accept any payment for his work. 'You're welcome,' he said – '*bevakasha*,' and walked off slowly back towards the checkpoint.

In the deepening dusk I soon got lost. With what was always my unreliable sense of direction, and that ever-changing layout of roads, it was impossible not to. Roads marked on the map were closed; other roads did not appear on the map. Two that we took came to an end in piles of boulders and heaps of earth, and a third in a high fence and closed gate, heavily guarded by soldiers and jeeps. In the end, we followed the direction of the rest of the traffic, and were soon stopped at a roadblock. Ahead of us, a man was ordered out of his car. Soldiers turned him against the side of the barrier kiosk; with two guns trained on him, he was roughly searched, his pockets emptied.

The other soldiers gestured us through impatiently. I drove on, looking for some sign, any sign of a familiar name or landmark or direction. We were in volatile Arab East Jerusalem and its constellation of villages. We were in the West Bank, in the dark, without access to a phone, utterly lost. I'd taken my fourteen-year-old daughter into danger, and I was terrified.

I wondered what I had done in my reactive, would-be liberal naivety. I remembered getting lost in East Oakland in California in the mid-1990s, at the height of the crack-fuelled gang wars, when the city had the highest homicide rate in the US. I was in a part of the inner city, the ghetto, where to show that you were lost, to stop and ask for help, or even to stop and look at the map was a reckless invitation to become another murder statistic. Now, as then, all veneer of liberality peeled away. I was in Arab territory and I was therefore in danger. I had forgotten the man who had helped me just a short while before – an Arab, a Palestinian; I had forgotten the man who had been my host, a man who was considerate, critical, funny, protective – an Arab, a Palestinian. I had forgotten my friend Mohamed in Cardiff, who always insisted I phone as soon as I got home, no matter how late, so that he would know I had arrived safely – an Arab, a Palestinian. I was a Jew, I was in hostile Arab territory, and I was in danger, so when I saw a sign for the Jewish settlement bloc of Ma'ale Adumim, and then that symbol of settler ideology itself rose up glimmering, white and pure on the hillside like some kind of heavenly offer of refuge, I was flooded, irradiated with relief. A Jewish settlement. A Jewish settlement city! My staggering, agitated heart steadied into a painful, hopeful pounding. Never mind that I hated what it was, the ideology it represented: it was *Jewish*, and we were safe…

I was not able, afterwards, to work out where we had gone, or why, or what kind of detour we had taken. It may have been a mere ten minutes, or an hour of driving, lost and afraid. When, later, I told Myriam the story of the puncture, rendering it comic, gliding over my stupidity, grateful for the kindness of a stranger who would accept nothing more than a thank you, she said grudgingly: 'Nu, so there are some good Arabs.'


Now, a year and a half later, Myriam is more afraid than when David was alive, more intemperate in her characterisation of Arabs. I tell her I'm going to Ramallah to meet Ghaith's mother, who might be able to help me find out where refugees from Al Murassas and Yubla ended up, and again she thinks I should not go. She reminds me how I got lost last time, what could have happened, though nothing happened. She is afraid for me: the West Bank is dangerous, and Arabs are not to be trusted. For Myriam, 'Arabs' are an undifferentiated mass that includes Palestinian citizens of Israel, Palestinians in the West Bank and Gaza, and the populations of the surrounding countries. She has welcomed me as she always does – with food, with heaps of food, with warmth and humour. And as always I am caught between some liberal imperative to challenge her prejudice, and my moral obligations as her guest. In the face of hers, my own fears and prejudices seem almost benign, but I don't challenge her; I swallow my outrage at her statements about Arabs. Instead we talk, in our usual mixture of Hebrew and French and English, about safer subjects – my uncle's death; my cousins' difficulties; my sister's death; how my parents are managing in their retirement in Australia; my own daughters coming and going between Wales and America.

From Tel Aviv I take the bus to Jerusalem, and another to Ramallah, where, over a lunch of chicken, pita and cold lemonade, Randa, Ghaith's mother, agrees to try to help put me in touch with refugees from Al Murassas and Yubla, if she can find them. She works in economic development with refugee groups. 'Look, *yani*, it's important that the story is told,' she says. 'I can help you, of course. But, *yani*,' she adds, 'you should keep in mind what the situation is. I've been in the camps here, and in Lebanon. You have three or four generations in one room, and all they have, *all* they have is their memories, and a wall painting of the village they came from. Jewish, Israeli... it makes no difference. For them a Jew, a Zionist, an Israeli – it's all the same. *Yani*, you should not say you're Jewish, that you have any connection with the kibbutz, with the place. Say, at the start, only that you're British...'

She asks me to write something for her, on letterhead, something formal to show my credentials and institutional affiliation, but I can't do that: this is a private quest, a personal search. I'm not an academic, a university employee

– I work for the Welsh Books Council, and my search is no part of my job. I have nothing to give her, to explain my intentions, to legitimise me, to show my trustworthiness and authenticity. Nevertheless I need her, or someone like her. I can't just take a bus across the border to Amman or Irbid or some other Jordanian city, ask for directions to the refugee camp, and go wandering through alleys, gazing at graffiti and martyrdom posters, hoping for an accidental meeting with the granddaughter or grandson of someone from Yubla or Al Murassas. I need intermediaries, with their particular judgements and opinions, and my intermediary will always need some evidence with which to reassure people who would rightly be mistrustful. Between me and Abu Omar there was my uncle. Between me and some possible refugees, Randa, or someone else – an UNRWA official, an academic, a peace worker, a political activist; some intro-ducer or stringer, some fixer or interpreter. But after meeting Abu Omar's grandson I am not sure about my intentions anymore. His after-image smiles at me, ironic, dimpled. Precisely why I am interested in meeting refugees from Al Murassas or Yubla, and precisely what I hope for, isn't something I want to dwell on anymore, is not something I am comfortable examining too closely.

Randa is interested in what I want to do, but my explan-ation of how I came to know about the villages so late upsets her. 'It's a crime to steal a people's history,' she says. 'My grandmother, in Jaffa, was the first in all of Palestine to own a piano. How can you say there was no one here, that there was no culture, just a few Bedouin?'

Before the first Intifada, Randa still used to be able to drive with her father from Jaffa to Gaza. Along the way he would point out all the sites of empty or destroyed Palestinian settlements, identifying them by their sabra thickets – the names, and who had lived there, and what had happened there. Soon, she says, that memory will be gone.


'How was it, then?' Myriam asks when I come back from a few days in the West Bank and Jerusalem. 'What's Ramallah like?' My cousin Eyal is also interested: he has only been there as a soldier, never as a visitor.

I think about the new Ramallah house where Ghaith's family lives, its five sleek storeys with a bathroom on every floor, a hot-tub downstairs, and bright, blocky designer furniture. They have their own swimming pool in the garden. I think about a bus I took from Bethlehem; its front bumper was hanging off, and the gearstick was wrapped in yellow electrical tape. A pregnant woman near me retched repeatedly into a pink plastic bag, and behind me two sick children were crying; one kept coughing and choking, and his drink splattered over the stained, sticky floor and ran down under the seats. At the checkpoint all but the woman with the children were asked to get out. As we waited for the soldiers to check us against our IDs, the pregnant woman leant her head on a concrete barrier post and moaned.

My aunt is watching me. 'It's complicated,' I say carefully.

On the bus back to Jerusalem from Ramallah, in the seats across from me, I watched a girl painting her mother's nails a deep maroon. When the bus reached the Qalandiya checkpoint, all of the men and most of the women rose from their seats and walked to the front and down the steps. They straggled along towards the processing hall, with its turnstiles and steel barriers. The bus driver waited while two soldiers conversed outside the open door. Eventually one of the soldiers turned to the bus, put a foot on the bottom step and heaved up her weight to lean in through the door, calling '*te'udot*'. The remaining passengers held up their blue East Jerusalem identity cards, and I, redundantly, my maroon passport.

On the far side of the checkpoint, the bus stopped again. The girl was tightening the lid on her nail varnish, and the women gathering their bags. The driver explained that he had to wait for the others, and pointed out a nearby bus that would leave sooner. I followed the other women to the new bus. In the seat in front of me, the woman held out a hand to her daughter again. For a short way the road was smooth, and the girl painted with a concentrated speed. Once we left the bit of even road by the separation wall, the drive became too rough and the mother turned away from the girl to look out the window.

Casually and implacably, despite the mundane brutality and banal oppressiveness of that architecture of power, small, irritable, human needs continued. The individual and the nation had shrugged a little, uncomfortable in this new concrete and razor-wire outfit, and then adjusted, and now it is out of sight for most Israeli Jews, and genuinely out of mind. Israeli citizens are not supposed to go to Palestinian-controlled areas of the West Bank. But now my aunt is reluctantly curious. 'What do they say about us, then?' she asks. 'Do they hate Israel? What do they think of us, your friends?'

I think of the Sno Bar, where I met Ghaith, out near a new Ramallah neighbourhood being built on the hillside. We drank Taybeh beer; our chips were served with plastic packets of ketchup and mayonnaise. 'I see the boycott of Israeli goods is in full swing here,' I'd said, turning over the mayonnaise packets. They were made by the Israeli company Ossem, which owned the factory at Kibbutz Beit Hashita.

The Sno Bar was full of 'internationals'. Ghaith and his

father complained about there being more internationals than Palestinians in Ramallah. The employees of NGOs and the UN, Ghaith said, earned two or three times the wage of local people, although it was local people who trained them and did the real work. His father had snorted with disgust. In one way, in the matter of restricted visas, he said, he was in agreement with the Israeli government. If people worked here, they should spend their money here, instead of buggering off to relax on the beach in Tel Aviv.

The peace process was a lucrative business, the Palestinian Authority a sham. 'We should dismantle the whole thing,' Ghaith said. 'The PA is doing Israel's dirty work; the whole thing is corrupt.'

I am not sure how to present this to Myriam. Whatever I tell her will reinforce what she already thinks. 'They have their own attitudes,' I say, hedging. I don't tell her about the divisions of wealth and poverty, about the tension in East Jerusalem; I don't mention going to Bethlehem, or getting lost in Hebron. 'Ramallah is full of internationals,' I say. 'UN, NGOs – it's very safe, very quiet.' I intended to reassure her, to say something neutral, but the word 'internationals' acts as a trigger.

'Why do they all go there?' she exclaims angrily. 'Aren't there other places? Why do so many people go to help the Palestinians? Why not Darfur, Somalia?' This leads her to the newer unhappiness over African asylum seekers. Every day hundreds cross into Israel, she tells me. 'And they're not really refugees. They just hear Israel is easy, and they come here for work.'

I hesitate, yawing at the edge of the gulf that we pretend isn't there, but which lies split open between us. Whether I keep silent or speak, neither will close it up. As always, as her guest, I struggle with my obligation to respect her hospitality. I understand what has sparked her reactions. My cousin has just been laid off, and he and his wife have three children to support. My other cousin is barely holding on to a part-time job in an old people's home. She is a single parent with three children. Myriam is trying to help with what little she has left of her pension – making mortgage payments, buying them a car, and providing frequent child-care. Of course she resents resources going to others; of course she wants to protect jobs, even though migrant workers and refugees are not taking jobs that Israelis want to do: they are taking the low-paid work that Palestinians used to do before the Intifada, before the closure of the border with the West Bank.

Myriam is afraid, and angry, and alone. She is in pain, and anxious about my cousins, and still grieving over my uncle David's death. My simultaneous feeling of outrage and sympathy settles into a leaden helplessness. It doesn't matter what I say – it doesn't make any difference. Why point out that Jews have been refugees, too, and migrant workers, and economic migrants; that migrant workers and asylum seekers are the same the world over? What purpose would it serve to tell her about the settlers' rubbish thrown down on the market in Hebron, or the pregnant woman leaning her forehead on a concrete post, groaning, while soldiers examined ID cards at the checkpoint? And why tell her what the security guard said to me at the central bus station when I got back to Tel Aviv? She might have said the same thing. He was young, Ethiopian, wearing a kippa. I waited till last to go through, as there was no X-ray machine and I thought I might need to unwrap and show him things I'd bought in Jerusalem. I explained that I had been shopping in the shuk.

'Any weapons?' he asked, taking me for a resident.

'No, no weapons,' I said.

'There have been a lot of Arabs today,' he said, giving my bag a cursory poke and handing it back. '*Loads* of Arabs.'

To say nothing to Myriam might be an acquiescence to attitudes that appal me, but to object is a pointless provocation, and, I know privately, grossly hypocritical. I am capable of hostility, too, whatever my liberal intentions; I have been inculcated in the same way, and have some of the same responses. My prejudices and fears are not so very different from hers, even if I handle mine in other ways.

There is a simplistic anti-racist dogma that demands you confront prejudice wherever you encounter it, but encountering it in yourself requires something else. Perhaps it's a life-long struggle that you can't ever win, but you go on doing battle anyway. And perhaps you get tired of the battle, you become exhausted, you can no longer be bothered – or the circle of your care shrinks and shrinks. You cannot simply undo the deep fear you learned as a child – it rises up uncontrolled when you feel threatened or at bay. You respond instantly, unwittingly, to the patterns that burned into you, patterns you are hardly aware of because you were exposed to them so young, like the wasp's warning colours and dreadful mask. I was stung when I was three or four years old, several times; there is a good, learned reason for my fear of wasps. That man tried to assault me when I was ten, so perhaps there would be good reason for a mistrust of men – and for an extreme aversion to Y-fronts. But he was Arab; I knew that without being told. I had already learned my apprehension of 'Arabs' from others, before that event – from a hand tightening on mine, from my grandfather's scar, from bullet casings and razor wire on the beach, and from half-heard news stories about the PLO. I don't blame my parents. Their fear was learned in childhood too, cumulative and unconscious, and reinforced in adulthood, and during their army service. Their learned apprehension is something they too have struggled against.

You can come to know how it operates in you, and why, to make conscious what lies dangerous and barely suppressed just below the surface. That's a defence, also, against imagining into being its opposite, too – the kind of sexual or political or cultural fetish I made, in an instant, out of Abu Omar's grandson. In that Romanticised, exoticised moment of desire, I endowed him with extraordinary properties, and dehumanised him utterly.

Perhaps this is why I could not afterwards remember his name. He could have no name, because he was a product of my need. He will always be beautiful in my memory, because he is other, because he is not-me, and because he represents my unconscious fears and desires, a dangerous terrain that I am afraid to know too well.

What can I say to Myriam? I know that if I were to describe the hospitality I received from Abu Omar, from Randa and Ghaith, she would surely say, as she said about the man who changed my tyre the previous year, 'Nu, so there are some good Arabs.' It would not affect her feelings about the undifferentiated mass of 'the Arabs'. What I am doing and where I have been travelling is a provocation to her – and it is therefore harder, and it costs more for her to offer me hospitality than for me to accept it. She welcomes me into her home despite what she herself is appalled by in me, despite what I am doing, which to her is treacherous and dangerous. She must be raw with aggravation, but she does not tell me to go and never come back – I am family. She welcomes me because hospitality is, to her, something unbreakable. Also, I realise, quite suddenly, quite unexpect-edly, that she loves me. I watch her, sitting exhausted and shrunk in the huge chair, with her tired, angry face, and she looks up at me and gives me her ironic, lopsided smile and that ineffable Israeli shrug, and the breach, the gulf, is sealed up, and none of it matters, because I love her too.

# 4 – Telling tales

My mother's younger sister, Hamutal, lives in Eilat, a resort city at the northernmost tip of the Red Sea. She's a scientist, a researcher in plant senescence. When I travel south to visit her, she gives me a tour of the labs and the experimental date palm plantations where she works just north of the city. I understand her explanation of senescence in an approximate way, as a metaphor for my own questions – what makes a thing die? It's not so much a question of what process kicks in so that it stops regenerating, as what process ceases, and why. What about love – what makes it end? What makes it slow down and stop? Or what process stops, making it impossible to go on – a habit of denial, a loss of will? In her fifth-floor apartment she has dates in the fridge that are still fresh and edible long after they should have begun to deteriorate. I hesitate, uneasy, when she offers them to me to eat.

The last time I stayed with Hamutal I was eighteen. It was late August, and I was heading back to England after eight months in Israel, but I wanted to go back with a tan, so for four days I burned myself in the desert sun, which at midday reached 50 degrees. Now, more than twenty years on, down on the beach, as if nothing has changed, the Heineken Bar is still blasting 'Mama mia, here I go again, Ah, Ah, how can I resist you...'

I buy an iced coffee at the beach bar, and find an isolated bit of sand, away from the hotel crowds, to spread out a towel. A few minutes later, coming ashore after a brief swim, I stand up without first looking where to put my feet, and tread on a sea-urchin. Caught in the thrum of its deep, throbbing pain, something goes still and quiet inside me. For a moment, I know exactly what James Wright meant when, in his poem 'A Blessing', he wrote that if he stepped out of his body he would break into blossom.

At the hospital gate, the security guard checks my bag. 'You cut your foot?' he says, seeing that I am limping.

'Sea urchin,' I explain. He shakes his head, not understanding, and stands back for me to pass.

The triage nurse asks what is wrong, and I show her my foot.

'What are you doing here?' she says. 'Go home and put your foot in a bowl of water. Twenty minutes – soak it in fresh water for twenty minutes; it's all you need.'

As I limp back past the barrier, the security guard says, 'Finished so quick? *What* did you do?' I slip off my sandal and show him the purple-black lines of broken-off spines in my foot. 'Why you didn't tell me?' he says. 'What you need is lemon.'

The other guard comes over. 'What she did do?' he asks in English. He too looks at my sandy, purple-barbed foot. 'No,' he says. 'What you need is to piss on it.'

I catch a cab back up the hill, to the tall apartment building where my aunt lives. When I was a child, this building stood on the boundary between the town and the desert. Now the city has grown well beyond it.

The cab driver pulls up to let me out. He is from France, and has been delighted I know some French. 'Tell me your name,' he says, as I take out my wallet.

Not again, I think – another marriage proposal. It is getting a little predictable. Earlier, in Tel Aviv, a Greek cab driver looked at me with bulging eyes in the rear-view mirror. 'What are you doing just visiting?' he said in English. 'You should come here to live with me.' When I told him why I was in Israel, he exclaimed, gesturing, both hands off the wheel, 'Israel must-to-be-strong; Israel must-to-be-a-Jewish-state.' Some of his best friends were Arabs, he said, but, in case I had not understood, he repeated 'Israel *must-to-be-strong.*'

Another cabdriver, mournful, pointed to the picture of his dead wife hanging from his rear-view mirror. 'She was a good woman,' he said me. Then, turning his head to look at me, he asked, 'What are you doing here? You should come here to live. You should marry me and stay – that's what you should do.' He'd just avoided a stalled truck by driving half on the pavement. *Please watch the road*, I wanted to say.

Two days later, it had been an Iranian cab driver, about fifty. 'You're a beautiful woman,' he said. 'Why are you single? You should not be single. Will you marry me and take me back with you to Wales?'

Cab drivers are always watching. They are truth tellers, messengers, Mercury figures: they know things about their new homeland, a few days after they arrive, that people born and raised there will never have an inkling of. Watching you, they know all your secrets. I hand this one my fare of fifteen shekels, and open the door. The heat blasts into the air-conditioned interior.

'Wait,' he says. 'Listen, I'm a fortune teller. Tell me your name, and your birthday, and I'll tell you your fortune.'

I pull the door shut again. 'Why do you need my name?' I ask.

'For the *gematria*,' he says. 'You understand? *Numérologie.*'

'OK,' I say. I give him the Hebrew version of my name, Yasmín, and my date of birth. 'But that's no good,' I add. 'I don't know my birthday in the Jewish calendar.'

He waves his hand dismissively. 'It's OK,' he says. 'I can translate it. Just a moment...' and he tilts his head and closes one eye. I wait, as his lips move. Then he opens his eye and turns back to me. 'You have had some difficulty with your father?' he asks.

'No,' I say. 'Not particularly.'

'Don't worry,' he says, ignoring my answer. 'It will be better. Everything will be better. Within the year you'll have money. And by your birthday you'll have love, a man.'

'Which year?' I say. 'The Jewish year?'

'It doesn't matter,' he says. 'By March.'

Up in the flat, I fill a basin and take it into the spare room. I sit down at the computer, with my foot in the water, to look up what should be done about a sea-urchin sting. I am not convinced by the triage nurse's quick dismissal, but the information I find online is alarming and contradictory: urine, fresh water, salt water, surgery, the necessity of removing all spines or risking nerve damage... Panicked, I stop reading. I look at my foot. As soon as it's out of the water, it begins to throb with pain. The sole is speckled now with black dots like seeds of a sabra fruit.

It hurts terribly, but when I submerge it again, the throbbing pain recedes, and I sit like that all afternoon. Forced to stop, completely, for the first time in days of travel and enquiry and observation, suddenly I am sick of it all. I am tired of everything: of trying to explain myself, of anxiety, of the constant duality, of being careful what I say. I am tired of struggling in my clumsy, childlike Hebrew, of making mistakes, of the brash aggressive noise of Israel, full of beautiful forbidden young men and lonely immigrant cabdrivers, and above all I am tired of my own loneliness and need.

The fortune the cabdriver has offered me is a painful one. He watched me; he recognised what I was. So did the others. And was it so evident? He asked if I had some difficulty with my father, and I said, 'No, not particularly,' but that was a lie. I do have some difficulty with my father. It was because of him that my mother left – I am certain of it. It was because of him that I was born in England, not Israel, because of him that I keep returning and leaving, unable to stay, unable to stay away. One moment down there on the beach, stung, startled, I thought I might break apart with love, and the next moment all light descends into doom and dark endings. Suddenly I can't wait to leave.

As soon as I leave, I am homesick; I want to go back. It always happens, every time. This time, however, I have brought home with me stories, photographs, papers and memorial books from the kibbutz archive, and when I piece the history together, when I find out almost by accident how the kibbutz was founded, I am not sure I ever want to go back again. My grandfather, it emerges, was not what I had thought him, and nor was the kibbutz. Though its members would no doubt vigorously deny it, the kibbutz was complicit in the displacement of hundreds of people from the Jezreel Valley – not during the war; not during the lead-up to the war, but a decade and a half earlier.


At home again, away from it all, I read voraciously – everything I could find about that place and what had happened there. So many Western travellers have written accounts of that small part of the world, the Jezreel Valley with its biblical past, that I was spoiled for choice – but all of them, every one, was unreliable: I could trust nothing that I read.

In the nineteenth century, dozens of European and

American Christian Bible tourists went travelling nervously along the route from Jerusalem to Nazareth, passing through Nablus and Jenin, and stopping in the Jezreel Valley at Nain and Mount Tabor on the way. These Western traveller accounts provide evidence, if read selectively (the bare open plains, without a village in sight), for the popular and inaccurate Zionist claim that Palestine was mostly empty before Jews began to arrive in larger numbers in the 1880s, and that the new arrivals created opportunities for work and profit, which attracted immigrants from surrounding Arab areas.

The land between Ein Harod and Beit She'an was marshy and malarial; tension between Bedouin tribes and the Arab tenant farmers was high, and nomads often raided the small agricultural settlements. In 1855, Bayard Taylor described the Jezreel Valley, in *The Lands of the Saracen*, as one of the richest areas in the world, a green sea of wheat and barley and grazing tracts with numerous sheep and goats. The Reverend John Mills, writing home to the Calvinistic Methodists in Welsh in 1858, described the abundance of Indian corn, and the beautiful peace and silence of the valley, despite recent depredations by roaming Bedouin raiders. Mark Twain saw it rather differently: he rode along the pilgrim route in 1867 and mocked the view of the Plain of Esdraelon, a chessboard of fields with white villages at its edges, as 'almost beautiful'.[3] Satirising pictur-esque steel-engraving depictions of the Middle East, he found particularly noteworthy the flies, rags, and every-where the weeping sore eyes of endemic trachoma.

It was Tristram, however – that naturalist-clergyman whose *Fauna and Flora of Palestine* had first seduced me – who proved most reliable. Unlike most of the nineteenth-century religious sightseers, Tristram travelled off the regular pilgrim and holy sites routes in search of geology, fauna and flora, and, above all, birds. Like other Western travellers in Palestine in the 1870s, he mentions the marauders, but also usefully observes that settlements in the Jezreel Valley were built for protection at the edges of plains and in the crevices of mountains, rather than exposed and vulnerable to attack in the open. His account shows very clearly that it was far from empty.

Tristram first went to Palestine in 1858 for his health, and returned for ten months of travel in 1863 and 1864, from which many of his books on Palestine derive. Armed and righteous, carrying letters of safe passage, he rode on horseback through the Jezreel Valley, breezily ascribing biblical origins to architectural remains and wells, navigating by reference to 'Judg. vii.22' and 'I Kings iv.', or 'Josh xxi.25' and 'Judg. v.23', recounting anecdotes of Arab sheikhs and tribes, of raiding a black vulture's nest, and shooting sunbirds, of feasting on lamb in Agyle Agha's hospitable tent, and retiring after a day's journey to blow eggs and skin specimens.

Long before recent Jewish arrivals grafted their present to the deep biblical past by naming new settlements after the old ones – Ein Harod, Beit Hashita – clergymen like Tristram roamed the country, declaring such identifications with definitive authority, or, less frequently, with more scrupulous hesitation. Tristram returned to Palestine time after time, as though, like me, he couldn't stay away – but for him Palestine's past, like its birds, was simple. Along with other British members of the Palestine Exploration Fund who set out into the landscape in the late nineteenth century, equipped with instruments and tents, with guides and pack-donkeys and guns, he was in pursuit of a story of God, and science, and the aspirations of Empire. The past could be discovered and described, mapped and catalogued, like the specimens and species he obtained during his forays into biblical ruin. By the end of his life, he had a collection of twenty thousand bird skins, which he donated to the Liverpool Museum, and had several species named after him, including the grackle, though he was not always so successful. He claimed to have been first to identify the little Dead Sea sparrow, whose yellow and black throat stripe distinguished it as a unique species, but its Latin name carries no hint of his.

When Tristram wasn't making his observations down the barrel of his rifle, he was seeing everything through a biblical filter. He didn't doubt that grassy mounds in the Jezreel Valley were signs of antiquity, or that Ein Harod marked the site of biblical Ein Harod. In 1865, he tentatively identified the village of Al Murassas as 'Marusseh (?)', and mentioned the sight of several grassed-over ruined villages nearby, marked by darker green. By contrast, the neighbouring village of Kafra was not ruined but inhabited and apparently flourishing.[4] Ten years later, he was more confident about identifying Al Murassas 'through careful investigation', this time in biblical terms that also explained its ruinous state: it was Meroz, whose inhabitants had been denounced by Deborah in Judges 23. The curse was fulfilled, he concluded, for 'in the midst of the richest pasturage of Issachar, the place has long since perished and left but a name'.[5] Griffon vultures circled above Mount Tabor, and an eagle or two, at a most inconvenient distance for his gun. By then, in 1875, the neighbouring village of Kafra was also ruinous and empty, and Tristram nowhere mentions Yubla, the other village that my mother remembered.

Despite Tristram's omission of it, I didn't have to dig very deep to find out about Yubla. No one would have to, if they wanted to know about it: Walid Khalidi's *All That Remains* has been in print since 1996, and there you can read that Yubla was a named settlement in the Crusader period. So too was the nearby village of Kafra, and records for Al Murassas date much further back than Tristram's identification of the village – to 1596, when it was a farm that paid taxes to the Ottoman government. By the late nineteenth century it was a small village. And there were many more villages, a whole network of villages, most of which don't appear in European or American travellers' accounts, because they had no biblical significance, and weren't on the way to or from the sites in Tiberias or Nazareth or Mount Tabor or Megiddo. Nain, important in the Christian scriptures, is a disappointment to the Christian tourists; Kawkab al Hawa is sometimes identified as an alternate name for the Crusader castle of Belvoir – but Na'ura, Taibe, Tamra, Yubla, Al Bira, Danna, Al Hamidiyya, Jabbul, Qumya, Al Sakhina and many others beyond them, spreading east towards the Jordan, north towards Nazareth, west towards the coast, and south across Gilboa to Jenin are often not mentioned at all.

In contradiction to the simple linear narrative I learned as a teenager about a Palestine mostly empty until Jewish 'return', the population of the country swelled and shrank and swelled again in the late nineteenth century, when drought, locusts, repeated raiding, cattle rustling, and changes in Ottoman land laws all impoverished the subsistence farmers and seasonally resident Bedouin. But if the Ottoman administration was slow to provide military protection – safely sending troops after the raiders had gone, according to Tristram – the British military conquest of Palestine in the First World War imposed a new kind of order. Soon after the establishment of the Mandate in 1921, the British authorities set out to update the surveys and maps of the Palestinian population, natural history and geological resources that had been compiled as a forerunner of empire in the 1880s by the Palestine Exploration Fund, in which Tristram had taken part. To these records they added detailed surveys of land ownership – including the villages of the Jezreel Valley.

By the time my grandfather moved into the Jezreel Valley in the late 1920s, the Arab villages there were secured against marauders from across the River Jordan, and they were settled and thriving. But now the villagers, mostly tenants of land owned by wealthy families in Haifa, Beirut and Damascus, were struggling with a new, more invisible threat. This was a threat against which they had no protection: the sale of the land they farmed to Jewish land companies, which in turn passed ownership of the land on to the new neighbouring Jewish settlements, and to other Jewish settlements-in-waiting, which included Beit Hashita.

It was disorientating to read the history of that place from this other perspective – to read not a heroic tale of tough pioneers and peasant workers, my grandfather among them, but a story of communities embattled by those new arrivals, these back-to-the-land Jews with their new technology and alien agricultural methods and voracious land acquisitions. Jewish settlements sprang up throughout the valley during the 1920s and 1930s, and raiding and fighting between Arab and Jewish neighbours was continual until the war in 1948. In 1948, of those many Arab villages in the valley, all but a handful – Na'ura, Taibe, Nain, Shulam, and Tamra – were emptied, and almost all of them were later destroyed.

I found it almost impossible to trust any account of what happened to the villages. It wasn't that the historical material itself was contradictory, but the interpretation of it was, and is. Still, in many ways, however you interpret its causes and consequences, the facts tell their own clear statistical story. During the unofficial war before the declaration of Israeli independence, with the implicit or explicit collusion of the withdrawing British Mandatory authority, and then the open war after the establishment of the state of Israel on 15 May 1948, the inhabitants of the villages left in fear, or were threatened, or were expelled. From Yubla, two hundred and ten people fled. From Al Murassas, four hundred and sixty. From neighbouring Al Bira, two hundred and sixty; from Danna, one hundred and ninety; from Kafra, four hundred and thirty; from Kawkab al Hawa, three hundred; from Al Hamidiyya, two hundred and twenty; from Jabbul, two hundred and fifty; from Qumya, four hundred and forty. Those are the numbers I found in Khalidi's compendium – village statistics based on projected population growth from earlier British census figures. Other historians give slightly different numbers, but it does not, in fact, make any difference.

I tried to imagine the village where I live, with its forty or so houses, its approximately one hundred people, gone, and all the villages within ten miles of it emptied, too – Bronant and Swyddffynnon, Ystrad Meurig and Ty'n Graig; Llangwyryfon and Llanilar and all the hamlets in between: whole valleys empty, villages of two hundred or three hundred years' standing, or longer, with deep histories, with graveyards full of ancestors, falling into ruin, or blown up.

Almost 3,000 people fled the villages that lay within a few kilometres of the new Jewish settlement of Beit Hashita, but in total, some ten thousand people from the greater Beit She'an or Beisan area headed east across the river border as refugees. My mother had been right when she'd speculated, hesitantly, about where the inhabitants of Al Murassas and Yubla had gone: they had fled to Jordan, and they were never able to come back.

With the exception of Na'ura, Taibe, Nain and Tamra, almost all the villagers left in the struggle for control of the valley, when the Golani brigade of the Haganah, the new Israeli army, began its 'Operation Gideon' campaign. The biblical Gideon, following God's diktat on who should fight with him against the Midianites, had selected his men according to how they drank from the fountain at Ein Harod, near Gilboa – three hundred men who drank from water scooped up with their hands, and none who lapped at the water like dogs. With too numerous an army, Gideon and his men might have been able to claim the success of battle as their own, whereas with three hundred men instead of tens of thousands, the intervention of an egotistical God would be clear. The Golani brigade perhaps did not have the same divine help, but the biblical precedent marked every battle by the Haganah in that valley, just as the biblical precedent determined the naming of the Jewish settlements – Kibbutz Ein Harod, where Gideon's men had been selected, and my mother's kibbutz, Kibbutz Beit Hashita, the place to which the Midianites had fled before them.

. In the face of this modern conflict for control of the valley between the Golani brigade and the Iraqi forces under the Arab Liberation Army commander, Fawzi Qawuqji, the flight of the villagers was nothing like the early departures for summer or winter quarters in Beirut and Damascus by wealthy, urban Palestinian Arabs. Those property owners had somewhere else to go, and had decided to make themselves scarce, as they thought, until the trouble was over. In contrast, the people who left the villages were poor tenant farmers, labourers, and semi-skilled and seasonal workers. They bundled their belongings, picked up children, and left, abandoning their harvests and hurrying along the network of paths between the villages, and then on to the gravel road to Beisan, heading away from the fighting. From the valley, from village after village, from hamlets and farms, from stone houses, adobe houses, and the mud and cane homes of settled Bedouin, people fled. Hundreds left each village, some of which were conquered and occupied by Jewish forces, and some of which saw no military conflict at all.

I found Khalidi's compendium of statistics and village remnants devastating. It was far more compelling than the many historians' conflicting accounts, because it was inarguable. The numbers of communities that were destroyed, the description of rubble-filled wells, broken gravestones, the now invisible sites of schools and mosques, all expressed the raw truth of what had happened, in a way that no analysis about causes and consequences could do. But what happened in the villages, and why people left, is contested, and the number of villages included in the lists of those emptied in 1948 varies from historian to historian, from one end of the ideological spectrum to the other. To Ilan Pappe, Jewish settlement in Palestine was an act of Western colonialism, and the Palestinian Arabs who became refugees between 1947 and 1949 were victims of a deliberate, carefully implemented Jewish ethnic cleansing plan to de-Arabise the new Jewish state. By contrast, Benny Morris, a defender of the Zionist project and founding ideology, though one of the first Israeli historians to document the flight of Palestinian refugees, attributes the cause of that flight to war (later, he acknowledged that it was a form of ethnic cleansing, although extraordinarily he defended this as being preferable to genocide). But Khalidi's book, *All That Remains*, gives a detailed account of the history, population and remains of each of the villages emptied between 1947 and 1949, and cumulatively, the scale and extent of that depopulation is shocking to read.

By now there are about five million Palestinian refugees – those who fled the newly established Jewish state in 1948, and their descendants. Unlike in Syria and Lebanon, Jordan granted citizenship to most of its Palestinian refugees, but some one and a half million still live in refugee camps, now urban ghettos, throughout the Middle East.

And those who fled east from the Jezreel Valley because of 'Operation Gideon', those who fled Al Murassas and Yubla, and the other nearby villages – where did they go? According to Saul, a member of Kibbutz Beit Hashita, they fled to Irbid, in northern Jordan, vanishing practically overnight immediately after Israeli statehood was declared.

Saul's account of 1948 appears in a collection of interviews about Beit Hashita conducted in the late 1970s and published in *Kibbutz Makom: Report from an Israeli Kibbutz*, by the sociologist Amia Lieblich. My mother had sent me the English edition of this book years before, and I'd hardly looked at it, and then forgotten I even had it. But when I got home from Israel this time, I took it down from the shelf, blew off the dust, and read all that had been there, available for me to discover long before, had I been interested, had it occurred to me to even look.

*Kibbutz Makom* was published in Hebrew and English editions in 1982. On the flyleaf of my mother's copy is an inscription to her in the neat Hebrew handwriting of her stepmother: 'To Anat, from the place of your birth, for your birthday – from your father and Shlomite, Beit Hashita, 1982.'

In the early 1980s, before the first Intifada changed Western attitudes to Israel definitively, interest in the kibbutz experiment – particularly as it pertained to the communal raising of children – was still high, but Lieblich's interviews reveal many of the tensions and difficulties. 'Kibbutz Makom' – meaning 'place' – is a pseudonym, as are all the names of the interviewees, but in my mother's copy, Shlomite had pencilled in the true names, including that of my grandfather.

The first section of the book concerns the earliest days of the kibbutz, and the memories of its oldest founder members provide a stark account of the hardships the kibbutzniks faced at the beginning, both ideological and physical. The founding of Beit Hashita followed the typical pattern of Jewish settlement in the Jezreel Valley: the building of a hasty tower-and-stockade structure, and the pitching of tents; then a few huts, shared rooms, a makeshift shower. For nearly seven years, members of the Beit Hashita *kvutza*, the founding group of the new settlement, had waited, camped, at nearby Kibbutz Ein Harod, for the Jewish National Fund to purchase land for the future kibbutz. At last, in 1935, thirteen years before the 1948 war, they were able to take possession of the new land bought on their behalf.

In the early days of the kibbutz, there was no money, no income. The valley was swampy in places, and malarial, and malaria cycled through the kibbutz 'pioneers'. Many died in the first few years; others, in despair at the hardship, the reality for which their political ideology had not prepared them, committed suicide.

The fields had to be cleared of rocks, wells dug and citrus

and olive groves planted, but there was no financial support, so some of the founding members went elsewhere in search of work in order to bring in money for the new community. In *Kibbutz Makom*, Saul and other founding members describe the terrible poverty and hardship, how they all lived in mud and tents and then flimsy little huts, clearing the land and building with their bare hands and only rudimentary tools. The strict communitarian social structure, in which everything was owned collectively, was expressed most acutely by 'Storehouse A', where new arrivals relinquished everything they owned and wore, and each member was allocated a parcel of clothes and a pair of shoes for the week.

When, at seventeen, I had gone to Kibbutz Regavim to do my ulpan, we too had cleared fields of rocks; we too had laboured on the land, redeeming its stony stubbornness, as we thought, like those early pioneers: and I, not so much new immigrant as returning kibbutz daughter, was walking in my mother's footsteps, my grandparents' footsteps, experiencing, like them, the nature of 'real' work. Reading those accounts of early hardship woke in me all the romantic adolescent longing of that peasant self-image.

The descriptions of fighting also fired in me again the drama of embattled heroics that I'd absorbed then: by day the kibbutzniks cleared fields, ploughed, irrigated, planted, built – shelters, the first children's house, a dining room, permanent showers. By night they fought off their neighbours, who came as intruders, raiders and saboteurs. It was the height of the Arab Rising of the 1930s, and members also served in the Palestine Police Auxiliaries, my grandfather among them. Interviewees in *Kibbutz Makom*, and accounts in individual memorial books that Tomer, the archivist, gave me, recall the early and endless conflicts with

Arab neighbours, the tense relationships, the deep mistrust, and the shady dealings. When Tomer told me what she remembered about the atmosphere of her childhood – the perimeter fence, the armed guards on the roof of the children's house – it all confirmed what I already knew, although I don't recall my mother telling me about it.

It was land that caused open conflict – the purchase and then cultivation by Jews of Arab land. From the beginning of the British Mandate onwards, land ownership and use was the most contested, fractious matter for the colonial authority, and efforts to control and legislate land owner-ship and land sales caused one kind of political uproar after another. Land ownership, and land-use rights, had changed under Ottoman law in the 1850s and again in 1871, and wealthy landowners, who lived at a distance, had possession of large estates in the area. They willingly sold land to Jewish land companies, which caused increasing landlessness among the fellahin, the Arab peasants. Under a new British land agreement in 1921, the tenant farmers of the Arab villages in the valley were in many cases able to register ownership for the first time. Some sold excess land; others were prevented from doing so, and tensions within the Arab community as well as between Arab and Jew grew and spread through the 1920s.

Although Beit Hashita initially acquired 3,500 dunams of land from the Jewish National Fund, it needed more, and expanded its holdings by buying from individuals in the neighbouring villages of Yubla and Al Murassas – or individual strips of land were bought, on behalf of the kibbutz, by Jewish land companies and the Jewish National Fund, which raised money from Jews throughout the world in order to buy land for the future Jewish state. Yosef Dagan, a founder member of Beit Hashita, was a representative of the Jewish National Fund. He negotiated over land with Al Murassas and Yubla. According to the account given in his memorial book, which my aunt Chaya gave me, he was an effective negotiator. There were quarrels with the villagers of Al Murassas, Yubla and Taibe and he calmed things down. He knew 'Arab etiquette', and spoke good Arabic. He understood what he called 'the mentality' of Arabs and family politics; he spent time with villagers, and knew who was poor, who was well off. If there was a financial crisis, this provided an opportunity to buy land, which he exploited. Among Arab neighbours he was seen as the kibbutz mukhtar, or chief – but no such role existed in the communist organisation of the kibbutz, with its egalitarian ethos and its endless committee meetings, discussions and unresolved ideological arguments.

It was Yosef Dagan whom Abu Omar had mentioned, when he recalled the understandings that were later to be reached in 1948 between the kibbutz and Na'ura. But the land the kibbutz obtained through Dagan's efforts was not contiguous. According to Saul, plots of land that the kibbutz cultivated alternated with plots of land owned by villagers, and conflict over field boundaries and use was both overt and covert – villagers' cattle were released deliberately or accidentally onto cultivated kibbutz fields; theft was rife, and kibbutzniks ploughed and harvested under armed guard, or at night, so as to avoid detection. Often land was bought from individuals in secret, and the right to use it was continually contested. Kibbutzniks and villagers knew one another, dealt with one another, and were often on friendly and civil terms, but they also fought with one another. In the 1920s and 1930s there was a continuous conflict between the new Jewish settlements and the Arab villages throughout the valley. There were bloody confrontations;

many people were injured and some kibbutz members were killed. Reading this, I hoped I might discover something about what had happened to my grandfather, but although Saul was no doubt recalling my grandfather's injury in one of these conflicts, he didn't name him.

Beit Hashita's experience was shared by the other Jewish settlements in the valley at that time. For Saul, remembering the conflicts, the provocation was mostly that of Arab neighbours 'trespassing' on kibbutz fields, or deliberately letting their animals destroy kibbutz crops. He remembered confrontations in which hundreds of Arabs fought against handfuls of Jews – bloody fights, with Arabs using stones and knives, which caused some serious head-wounds, my grandfather's among them.

But everything changed suddenly, overnight, on the 15th of May, 1948, according to Saul. That day, the morning after the midnight declaration of Israeli independence, he was working on the fields near one of the villages, driving the combine harvester, with some thirty armed guards nearby. Then he saw the mukhtar of the village leave his house and head his way (he does not specify whether it was the mukhtar of Al Murassas or Yubla). Clambering up on the combine, the mukhtar offered to sell the kibbutz his crops, and Saul 'knew' the conflict was over. 'Just the day before, just one single day, the same Arabs were so sure of their victory, so sure that they would soon be looting our property, that one of them said to me: "See the Arab-Iraqi army up there?" They were really close by. On the hills, I could see 300-400 men. "Their commander has maps of Tel Aviv." That's what he told me on May fourteenth.'[6] On May 15th, with independence declared, and with open war, the perpetual conflict between Beit Hashita and its Arab neighbours was over. That, at least, was how Saul remembered it.

It was no doubt convenient to pin those memories to such a definitive date: the account fits with the narrative of the embattled Jewish state, under attack after its legitimate declaration of independence. Inconveniently, the historical record tells a somewhat different story – the Gideon campaign had begun five days earlier in anticipation of the declaration of independence, and the larger military conflict had begun months before, and in some places the previous year, and it continued, with periodic ceasefires, until early 1949. But as far as the conflict with the kibbutz and its immediate neighbours was concerned, Saul's memory was accurate: soon, almost all the Arab neighbours of the kibbutz were gone.

After the end of the 1948 war, members of refugee families who had been separated during the conflict sent messages to each other across the border, in broadcasts on Jordanian and Israeli radio. Saul was told, though he didn't hear it himself, that a refugee from Al Murassas or Yubla, now living in Irbid, had dedicated a song to him on Jordanian radio. Twenty years later, after the 1967 war, when the borders were once more open, some of the refugees from Al Murassas and Yubla came back to visit. It was impressive, Saul remarked, how they had got on in Irbid – opening shops, 'their special talent', and sending members of the next generation, whom he'd known as babies, to study throughout eastern Europe as doctors and engineers. 'And all this, from a tiny village which hardly had a primary school,' he exclaimed. 'This development stems, perhaps, from their forced escape from here.'

Most of the Arab population had fled or been expelled, but some people remained in a handful of villages, and this created a moral issue that troubled Saul – that of Arabs working as hired labour on land that had once belonged to them. 'We took these fields from them – we took them in war and many kibbutz members were killed in those battles, mind you,' he said to his interviewer, but hired labour was anathema to him, to the kibbutz ideology: 'If we become employers, the kibbutz becomes an employer, our children become employers, and they will be like employers all over the world in spite of all our education ... And this will be the end of the kibbutz.'

This was the story of Al Murassas and Yubla, the villages my mother had named on the phone that day in late August when I sat on my doorstep in Wales, talking to her in Australia. The story is there to discover in *Kibbutz Makom*, in *All That Remains*, and elsewhere, and the larger context can be read in books on the 1948 war by Pappe, Morris, Avi Shlaim and many others. If the kibbutz was not directly responsible for what happened, it certainly benefited, for after 1948, Beit Hashita and its neighbours began to cultivate land that had belonged to the destroyed villages. But some of Beit Hashita's fields that had belonged to Al Murassas and Yubla were not the spoils of war: this was land that had been bought from the villages. And none of this explained the 3,500 dunams of land with which the kibbutz had started – none of it explained Shatta, which, in *Kibbutz Makom*, Saul describes casually as 'an old abandoned Arab village'.


A picture of Shatta hangs on the wall of the entranceway to the kibbutz archives – a long, framed, black-and-white photograph, with a Hebrew caption that reads *HaKfar Shatta: 1933*. In the foreground on the left, against Mount Gilboa, stand the squared, flat-roofed buildings of an Arab village; to the right the buildings are falling into a ruin of tumbled stone.

I could not find the name Shatta on the lists of Palestinian Arab villages depopulated between 1947 and 1949. It's not among Benny Morris's 369 villages in *The Birth of the Palestinian Refugee Problem*, not among Ilan Pappe's 531 depopulated villages in *The Ethnic Cleansing of Palestine*, and not on Salman Abu Sitta's maps in the *Atlas of Palestine* or in his *The Return Journey*. It isn't on the list of 418 depopulated villages in Walid Khalidi's *All That Remains*, either. Shatta doesn't appear in the record of conflict because it wasn't depopulated in the lead-up to the 1948 war, or during the war itself, or after. It was depopulated years before that, in 1931.

All that's left of Shatta is its hidden railway station building, lying out of sight inside Shatta prison, which is a converted Tegart fort from the British Mandate period. Now only the prison name retains a memory of the village. 'I looked before me and saw a huge building towering like an ugly demon of the desert,' recalls Saeed, the protagonist of Emile Habiby's novel *The Secret Life of Saeed the Pessoptimist*. 'Its walls were yellow, and around it there was a high, white outer wall. There were guards posted on each of the four sides of the roof, and they could be seen standing with their guns at the ready. We were awestruck by the spectacle of this yellow castle, so exposed and naked of any vegetation, protruding like a cancerous lump on the breast of a land itself sick with cancer. The big man was unable to control himself and exclaimed, "There! The terrible Shatta prison! How fantastic!"'[7]

This prison is one of the most evocative and terribly familiar landmarks from my childhood; this is the prison you pass just before turning left off the Ruler Road to Kibbutz Beit Hashita. By the time my mother was old enough to remember, in the mid 1940s, all that was left of the village itself was *beit ha-sheikh*, the sheikh's house – a building that had initially been used by kibbutzniks as a cowshed. It was unsafe, with precarious stone walls. As a child she and her classmates found broken pottery there, and they thought that it was from biblical times. 'But,' she said to me, correcting herself, 'I expect they were just bits of pottery from the people who had lived there before.' Her brother Asaf, fifteen years younger than her, also remembered *beit ha-sheikh*. By the early 1940s there were no other remains, and now *beit ha-sheikh* is also gone.

Taking down the picture for me to photograph, Tomer, the kibbutz archivist, told me that Shatta was the site of a biblical settlement: kibbutzniks had found ancient coins, which were now in a Tel Aviv museum. I wondered about my mother's memory of broken pottery. How old might it have been after all? Tristram also had little doubt that Shatta – or Shutta, as he spells it – was the site of biblical 'Beith Ha-shittah', mentioned in Judges 7:22.

The archive photograph of the village shows that parts of it were ruinous in 1933, but a good half of it was intact. 'When the village was destroyed,' Saul told his interviewer in the late 1970s, 'one building remained – a big house which we used as a barn. All the cows were kept in this house, and on the roof we built a wooden hut, where we lived.' No doubt this was the *beit ha-sheikh* of my mother's memory. But two years before that photograph was taken, Shatta was not in ruins, nor uninhabited: it was very far from being 'an old, abandoned Arab village'. In 1931 it had been thriving, and its residents did not conveniently get up one day and walk away, leaving it empty. Shatta was deliberately depopulated. It was not depopulated as a result of war or conflict, nor for strategic military or political reasons – it was depopulated in order for Kibbutz Beit Hashita to have its land.

It was in New York, by chance, that I found out the history of Shatta, when I was visiting my brother, who lives in the East Village. It was May, and already hot and sticky, and the parks were full of children and dogs. In some streets, I heard more Hebrew than English – there was an enclave of Israeli expatriates living there, and there were Israeli restaurants, shops, a humus cafe. I went into one Middle East import store to look at the tins of olives and pickles, as I always do – to see if they'd been canned in the Beit Hashita factory. They had. And in the cramped basement of a second-hand bookshop, I browsed the Middle East section as I always do, though I already had so much to read, too much to read. There seemed no end to the research I could do.

The usual books were there, the two extremes of inter-pretation sitting uneasily side by side: Ilan Pappe's *Ethnic Cleansing of Palestine*, and Joan Peters's *From Time Immemorial*. In his memoir, *Palestine, a Personal Story*, Karl Sabbagh describes *From Time Immemorial* as 'a wildly inaccurate account of the history of Palestine and one of the most comprehensively demolished non-fiction books of recent years'; decades earlier, Peters's Zionist apologia had deeply moved me, and reinforced my misapprehensions.[8] A little further along from Pappe and Peters there was an unprepossessing scholarly paperback, published, like Peters's book, in 1984. Neither its rather dull factual title – *The Land Question in Palestine, 1917-1939* – nor its cheap gloss cover, showing a dark, blue-washed detail of a Mandate-era map, were particularly striking. But the index was different. In the index I found Shatta. Not a footnote, not a passing reference, but many references: a discussion.

Unlike the history of Kibbutz Beit Hashita, which is available in *Kibbutz Makom*, Shatta's history is largely hidden, and you have to glean it and reconstruct it from fragments, passing remarks, remnants and asides. Nevertheless, Shatta was important: what happened there caused a stand-off between the British colonial authority and the Jewish Agency, the Israeli government-in-waiting – a stand-off from which the Jewish Agency had to back down. Shatta was in fact a test case for the British Mandate.

The outrages of 1948 and their aftermath, increasingly documented and discussed, have long since displaced the less obvious outrages of land transfers in the 1930s. Walid Khalidi's *All That Remains* is the definitive compendium of the 418 villages depopulated in 1948, but his criteria for inclusion are rigorous: it lists only those settled (not seasonal) villages that were inhabited at the start of the war and which lay within the 1949 ceasefire lines, and it therefore excludes Shatta. The village gets a single passing mention, in relation only to Al Murassas, which is described by Khalidi as being located four kilometres from Beit Hashita, 'established in 1935 on land purchased from the village of Shatta'.[9] But Beit Hashita wasn't established on land purchased *from* the village of Shatta – the village itself was purchased.

Shatta was settled and well established when Tristram roamed the area with his growing collection of birds' eggs and skins, and when Mark Twain rode sneering along the pilgrim route to Beirut. In the nineteenth century the Shatta railway station, now incorporated into the prison, was one of the valley stops on the short Haifa branch-line of the Ottoman Empire's great north-south railway. The Hejaz railway used to serve the huge expanse of land from Medina in the far south to Damascus in the north, and at Dara, a little south of Damascus, the branch line cut west to Beit She'an, and then through the Jezreel Valley to Afula (where another local line branched off south to Nablus), and on to Haifa at the coast. During the Mandate period there were stops all along the branch line through the valley, and the railway and its bridges were a frequent target for Jewish underground groups fighting against British colonial rule, both before and after the Second World War.

The building inside the prison, and the prison's name, is all that now remains of Shatta, because in 1931 the two hundred and fifty-five villagers had the village sold from under them by Raja Ra'is, a wealthy landowner who lived in Haifa. The buyer was the Palestine Land Development Company, an organisation that made purchases on behalf of the Jewish National Fund; in turn, the Jewish National Fund passed the land on to the founding group of Beit Hashita. But they had to wait, encamped at Ein Harod, for some years before the land sale could go through, my grandfather among them, because when it came to the attention of the British authorities, the sale of the village was blocked.

I stood in that basement bookshop in New York reading Stein's *Land Question in Palestine* with growing disbelief. I was shocked to find the story of Shatta. The language was plain, factual, technical, but the implications of Stein's discussion appalled me.

The story of the village is woven right through the story of land sales in the 1920s and 1930s in Stein's book. In 1919, two Haifa families had owned most of Shatta, but in 1931, in anticipation of the sale, a member of one family, Raja Ra'is, had bought a large share of village land from Anis Abyad, a member of the other family, thereby planning to augment his profits. But the land was 'encumbered' with tenants, and this meant that the seller would be obligated to pay compensation to those whom the sale dispossessed. The sellers could avoid paying such compensation if the land was free of tenants before the sale went through, and Ra'is intended to dispossess his more than two hundred tenants in Shatta, before selling the land into Jewish ownership. Unfortunately for him, but fortunately for the residents of Shatta, his timing was bad, as it coincided with the outcome of the British investigation into the 1929 Arab revolt, which left the colonial authority more sensitive to the problem of Arab peasants losing the land they farmed.

In the 1920s and 1930s, Arab organisations and powerful individuals lobbied for restrictions on the sale of Arab-owned land to Jews, and against increased Jewish immigration to Palestine, which was augmenting the demand and market for such sales. In counterpoint, the Jewish Agency, the Jewish quasi-government in Palestine, lobbied the Mandatory authorities and the British Government for increasing the Jewish immigration allowance, and against the restrictions on land sales. Those restrictions on immigration were seen, by sympathisers, as a terrible repudiation of Jewish suffering, particularly after Germany's Jews were stripped of citizenship. But the buying up of land for Jewish settlement had the most immediate and terrible effect on the Arab fellahin: they lost their livelihoods and their homes, so that others might have them.

The planned sale of Shatta land, and the intended dispossession of its tenants, caused a row between the British Mandatory authority and the Jewish Agency. The Jewish Agency was informed that if it did not prevent the eviction of Shatta's tenants, recent recommendations on restrictions in land transfers between Arabs and Jews would be implemented by the British authorities. Under this pressure, Chaim Weizmann, head of the Jewish Agency, had to capitulate, though he disclaimed Jewish responsibility for the intended dispossession of Shatta's tenants, and blamed the Arab landowner, Raja Ra'is.

In the end, there was a compromise: an arrangement was made for the two hundred and fifty-five inhabitants of the village to be resettled elsewhere and Shatta, conveniently 'disencumbered' and transformed into the empty Arab village of Saul's description, could be sold into Jewish ownership. The purchase went ahead in April 1931, but the British census of Palestine in that year recorded the village's population as it was before the village was sold: two hundred and fifty Muslims, three Christians and two Jews.

The black-and-white photograph of Shatta that I had seen hanging in the entryway to the kibbutz archive does indeed depict an empty village in 1933, but the villagers did not abandon it – it was they who were abandoned. This is what Beit Hashita was founded on. The kibbutz, an idealistic community with an ideology of self-sufficiency and communist equality, of workers owning the means of production, of worker empowerment, was made possible by dispossessing more than two hundred peasant workers.

My mother, like so many members of kibbutzim that were established before 1948, always stresses that these settlements were not built on stolen land, that the land was bought and paid for. That is my mother's story about Beit Hashita: the kibbutz was not a thief or a trespasser; its land was bought legally. But the legal argument provides no moral defence. Even if it was the wealthy Arab landowners and the Jewish Agency who colluded in the dispossession of Shatta's tenants, and even if the sale conformed to British colonial law, for an ideological community of social and political brotherhood, it was unethical and decidedly hypocritical, and the members of the new kibbutz, my grandfather included, were complicit in a moral crime.

Thirteen years after that sale went through, in 1944, when the British authorities in Palestine revised their estimates of the population and land ownership, only four dunams of Shatta's land were still Arab-owned, and its population of 590 was entirely Jewish, comprising the members of Kibbutz Beit Hashita. My mother was by then three years old, and her mother had already left the kibbutz and gone south to work by the Dead Sea. My grandfather, Yair, was in the army, based on the Mediterranean coast at Kibbutz Sdot Yam, near the Roman ruins of Caesarea.

On the second floor of the kibbutz archive, the walls are lined with rows and rows of dark wooden drawers, like a massive columbarium. There is a drawer for each kibbutz member who has died, containing a file of papers, photographs, and their *yiskor* or memorial book. To one side there is a memorial to the members who were killed in the many years of conflict since the founding of the kibbutz – the Lebanon War in 1982, the Yom Kippur War in 1973, the Six Day War in 1967, the Suez Crisis in 1956 and the War of Independence in 1948. Prominent in the memorial are the eleven who 'fell' in 1973. This was the largest number of deaths, as a proportion of the population, of any village or town during that conflict, a conflict the country almost lost, and which left a terrible scar of insecurity after the giddy success of the Six Day War.

When I visited, it was very still in the archive, and cool after the heat outside. Standing before that memorial, it struck me that it was not after all strange that as a child and teenager I had never wondered about my grandfather's scar, about his having been attacked by Arabs. It had been not only part of my accepted childhood landscape, but part of everyone's landscape there too: a history of conflict and fear, of attack and defence. With all those years of accumulated trauma, it was not very surprising that no one talked about it unless asked: the violence was normalised, unremarkable.

In his own accounts, published in his *yiskor* book, my grandfather Yair is humorous and self-deprecating about his experiences of danger and conflict. He describes his antics in the Palmach, the strike-force created by the Haganah, the Jewish army, during the Second World War, and labouring at the salt works in Atlit and Sdom, on the Dead Sea. He recounts walking all the way back from Jerusalem to the kibbutz, nearly getting lost, and nearly getting shot, and tells a story of guarding the railway line in 1948 at Beit Yosef, a nearby kibbutz, where he dug in as instructed. Dedicated and committed, he waited and watched for several days only to discover, when his commander eventually remembered he was there, that the war in that area had ended on the first day.

Before joining the Palmach he'd been a member of the Palestine Police Auxiliaries, originally employed by the British to guard the Jewish settlements, the kibbutzim and the co-operative farms against Arab attack. Under the tutelage of the controversial Colonel Orde Wingate, a British maverick, the Police Auxiliaries had been developed during the Arab uprising of 1936 into a strike force against bandits and insurgents: they mounted attacks, first on Arab settlements, and then across the northern border into Syria and Lebanon. They were not merely a defence organisation – they went on the offensive, too. When, during the Second World War, the Palmach was formed, only a limited number of kibbutzniks could join, and my grandfather had been one of them: he was in the sea cadets division, the Palyam.

Secretly the Palyam helped land illegal immigrants and refugees, smuggling them through the naval blockade when the British had placed limits on Jewish immigration. Later they helped to illicitly disembark camp survivors. My grandfather was in his twenties at the time. Mid-war, it must have had a fevered intensity, their risk-taking – but they were young, tough idealists, setting out from the tumbled ruins of Caesarea in small boats to lay mines or beach immigrant ships, wading the refugees ashore in the warm purple evenings, the lights from the young town of Tel Aviv perhaps visible to the south, of Acre and Haifa to the north. Closer yet lay Atlit, where the refugees who were caught were held in British detention camps. At the end of the war the Palmach was officially disbanded by the British authorities, but it was incorporated into the Haganah, the Jewish army that sometimes worked with and sometimes against the British, and would become the Israel Defence Force of the Jewish state.

Oral histories of the Palyam have been published on the website *palyam.org*, and it gives a vibrant picture of their activities in the mid-1940s, but it was in my grandfather's *yiskor* book, which I brought home with me from the archive, that I found an answer to the question that had first sparked my search: he'd written an account of being attacked and hospitalised in 1944.

He had travelled back from the coast to Beit Hashita that week to be at home for my mother's third birthday, on the 5th of July. That Saturday morning the commander of the kibbutz guards arrived with the urgent news that villagers from Yubla were attacking kibbutzniks out in the 'Yubla fields'. That's how, many decades after the event, my grandfather still described the place – as the 'Yubla fields'. The guards commander gathered together seven or eight men to fight them off, and my grandfather, with the others, grabbed some clubs, clambered into a van and drove out of the kibbutz and up to the fields. The kibbutzniks were outnumbered by villagers, and more men from the village were arriving. My grandfather was the first to reach them, and he hit a man with a club. He was surrounded and was himself clubbed over the head and lost consciousness, though he continued to be beaten after he fell. In that fight another kibbutznik, Shabo, was stabbed in the back, and they were both taken to the hospital in Afula.

My grandfather, along with Shabo, was charged – their hospitalisation was evidence that they had participated in the attack. The man from Yubla whom my grandfather had attacked had made a claim for compensation. My grandfather and Shabo stood trial before an English magistrate, who asked both defendants and accuser to show the evidence of their injuries. The man from Yubla rolled up his sleeve to show his broken arm; my grandfather took off his hat to show his head injury, and Shabo pulled up his shirt to show his knife wound. The magistrate, unable to clearly attribute blame, ruled that the injuries were equal, that it was tit for tat, and ordered them all to leave his courtroom.

Despite its terrible details, my grandfather's telling of the story is light-hearted and matter of fact. What first struck me about his account was not his violence. Instead, what sang out like a melancholy minor chord was the unstated fact of my mother alone on her third birthday. Behind it lay the incomparable loneliness of all those children, at three years old, at two, as babies, going to bed and waking up without their parents, brusquely seen to by inexperienced, tough young women who had numerous children under their care, women who were often reluctantly separated from their own children, and couldn't help but resent those for whom they were responsible. For my mother it was even worse: her own mother had left, her father was stationed away at the coast, and she was painfully shy among the other frightened children in that harsh, dangerous world of extreme poverty, violence, hard labour and strict ideology.

I had reconstituted my mother and my grandfather as some kind of noble Jewish peasants – but that, in its entirety, was a myth. As I found out from his *yiskor* book and the other archive papers, my grandfather had no peasant roots: he'd rebelled against his parents, who were well-educated members of the petit bourgeoisie, small-time capitalists, and he'd joined the kibbutz movement, committing himself through Labour Zionist ideology to its egalitarian hardships. And that's what the kibbutz movement was: an invented way of life, an invented tradition of working the land, driven, at its best, by idealism, and at its worst by a harsh ideology that could not admit its wrongs. Nor was there anything particularly gentle or noble about my grand-father – he had been assaulted, yes, and seriously injured, but he had initiated the attack. He had done so in defence of land he believed his community had a right to own, but I was not sure it had any right to it at all.

It was difficult to accept that the kibbutz movement was no peasant movement and never had been, and a shock to discover that my personal story, my family story, was a concoction, another lie. The kibbutz movement had at its heart a hypocrisy and contradiction, and all my hazy notions of its noble endeavour, and of my grandfather's noble peasant endeavour, burned away. The true peasants in Palestine were not the kibbutzniks like my grandfather, but the Arab fellahin, those tenant farmers whom the kibbutzniks had so casually and so easily displaced by capital in the 1920s and 1930s, and then by war in 1948.

Nevertheless, even then, after reading about Shatta in Stein's blue-covered, fact-stuffed book in that musty, humid bookshop in New York's East Village, even after the last romantic vestiges of my story of Israel and what it meant to me were torn up like that, I still could not quite let the story go, not entirely. The knowledge of where you come from holds you, like a parent. Grappling with it is part of the process of individuation. You might reinvent it, but you still circle back to it; you might reject it, cut yourself off from it, repudiate it – but that very rejection is part of what forms you. Even if identity is an elective story about the past and about place rather than an immutable, essentialist biological fact, on a day-to-day basis we still order one another and ourselves in relation to those stories of past and place as though they are not tenuous and contingent. 'Where are you from?' we ask, and, if we don't get a clear answer, or if we don't get one that answers the real question we're asking, we add: 'Where are your parents from? Where is your family from?' I know where my family is from, but now I am ashamed of that place, ashamed of the crime and the destruction on which it was built.

# 5 – Surveillance

As if to reinforce my doubts, the next time I went back, a year and a half later, Israel started to express doubts about me.

At the El Al check-in line at Heathrow I failed to navigate the security agent's usual questions – *Did you pack your bags yourself? Did anyone give you anything to carry?* – and the more specific, personal ones I've come to expect: *Where is this name from? This isn't a Jewish name...* Although my sense of identity is internally coherent, on approaching and on leaving Israel it looks stitched together, and I never quite feel able to establish legitimacy.

It was August 2009, and swine flu had at last displaced the aftermath of the war on Gaza in the news. Israel was in a panic over swine flu, perhaps more than other countries because of its unkosher provenance, because it carried the cultural taint of living at close quarters with unclean pigs. A religious group sent a party of rabbis up in an aeroplane to blow shofars and say prayers over Israeli airspace, in an attempt to keep swine flu out.

The agent wasn't satisfied with my answers. She asked me again for the family story, perhaps seeing if I would tell a different version. She asked me again what I meant by 'secular'. She asked me again why my mother had left, and why I had learned Hebrew, why I kept coming back.

The rest of the line was moving fast. Almost all the passengers were Israelis returning home after the summer. The agent left me standing by the airline's X-ray machine while she went to consult with a colleague. They glanced at me and turned away again, whispering, in a close huddle, as the queues beyond me shortened.

Waiting in a little cordoned-off isolation area, I was marked as dubious and suspect. Perhaps I had somehow violated the unstated agreement, the obedience demanded of you to pretend that you're hearing the security questions for the first time. Now a second agent was coming over. She stared at me a long time, and then back at my British passport, and then at my face again. She asked me the same questions. She asked me the second round of questions. She asked me new questions – about whether I marked the Jewish holidays, about synagogue attendance, about membership in any Jewish groups. Every answer *No... No... No...* made me feel less and less a Jew, more and more suspect. 'Since when was being a secular Jew a problem?' I wanted to ask. 'Israel isn't full of secular Jews?' People were staring. I suppressed my questions, my irritation, my rising paranoia.

'Tell me again,' she said, 'why you are going to Israel,' and when I lied, saying I was visiting family, she knew it. Though I was planning to see them, my main purpose was to go back to the village sites – and to go on to Amman, in Jordan, to meet Malik.

Malik was the grandson of a man who'd fled from Al Murassas, one of the approximately 10,000 people from the greater Beisan area who'd headed east across the Jordan river in 1948 and could not return. Malik was thirty, plump, and going bald. He listened to Julio Iglesias, and was getting married in the autumn. 'If you are doing some justified research, I am happy to help your good self,' he'd written. He'd agreed to see me in Amman if I could make it there, or to talk by phone.

Someone at Zochrot had put me in touch with Malik. Sooner or later, almost everyone who is beginning to doubt the Zionist version of the past ends up making contact with Zochrot. It's an NGO on the far left, and the people who work there are radical anti-Zionist progressives committed to social justice for Palestinians inside and outside Israel. Their funding comes from abroad, but this has not protected them from the increasingly intrusive efforts, through legislation and personal and media harassment, to restrict or stop their work. Zochrot also serves informally as a kind of clearing house for events, information and other groups to do with the Nakba, with the more general Arab history of Palestine – both that of Arab citizens of Israel, and Palestinians forced to leave – and with Israeli protests against occupation of the West Bank and Gaza.

Staff members at Zochrot had provided me with maps showing the sites of the destroyed villages in the area around Beit Hashita, and promised to try to make contact with people whose families had come originally from Yubla and Al Murassas. After some enquiries they'd sent me Malik's contact details, and Malik and I had exchanged emails and become friends on Facebook in the spring of 2009, in the long aftermath of the winter war on Gaza. The ferocious brutality of the war shifted public opinion definitively in the UK, and, close to home, in particular ways in Wales. Wales, itself disenfranchised, likes to ally itself with the disenfranchised elsewhere; not so many decades before, it had sympathised strongly with the national aspirations of disenfranchised and embattled Jews. That had been the subject matter of my doctoral dissertation. After the war on Gaza, the appalled dismay at Israel's actions and towards all Israelis became, for a period of time, intemperate, and spilled over messily into indiscriminate hostility, as would recur again and again in the years to come. Everyone was jumpy and defensive, and Israel's representatives abroad – politicians and paid propagandists, self-styled supporters and security agents – guarded the tightly controlled perimeter of Israel's borders, both physical and rhetorical, with extremes and absolutes.

The agent was watching me closely, and now she told me to wait. She disappeared through a back door with my passport in her hand. I wondered if I was being checked against a list, or being added to a list. The following year, when an assassination in Dubai revealed that Mossad had been harvesting British passports, I wondered if my passport details too might have been taken in just this way.

My fellow passengers, passing, looked at me with hostility and suspicion as I stood, conspicuous, in my roped-off space. They whispered to each other, particularly the women in their wigs and hats, whom I hated, suddenly, for their certainties and simplicities. The children were the worst: they stared, hanging off a parent's hand, or the luggage trolley. Belligerently I told myself I had nothing to hide – resentfully, sullenly, I thought I had as much right as they did to go to Israel, to get on the plane. Underneath was something else, and I could smell it coming up off me, a rancid smell – the beginning of fear.

At last the security agent came back through the door and pointed me out to a third woman dressed in a dark suit. The dark-suited woman walked over, brisk and efficient, with my passport in her hand. It was not questions now, but instructions. 'This is a random security measure,' she said, and I almost laughed at the absurdity. What was random about this? 'As part of this random security measure, we will need to take your hand-luggage and your suitcase.'

'My *hand*-luggage?' I said. I thought of what was in my

bag, and with a little internal shock wondered what would happen if they saw the maps, the trilingual reproductions from Abu Sitta's atlas showing the destroyed Palestinian villages in the Jezreel Valley. How would I account for them, and for the tape-recorder in my suitcase? What alternative, erroneous story of a security threat might they string together from such evidence? Or, indeed, what correct story might they deduce? *Family history research*, I could tell them; *just family history…*

The security guard was frowning at me now, impatient.

I knelt down and began to take what I most needed out of my bag.

'Is that all you have?' she asked, looking down and then away. She seemed embarrassed by the public display of my possessions on the floor. She hesitated a moment. 'OK, well, if that's all you have… Fine, take it with you, then, and we'll check it at the gate.'

I packed everything back into my bag, and she took my case away. All the passengers had gone and only one check-in desk was still open when at last I was free to go and pick up my boarding pass.

When, after passport control, I walked through the metal detector at airport security and set it off, my paranoia leapt up several levels. I had nothing metal on me – nothing at all. Had they been alerted? Had I been targeted? Did the label that had been stuck on my bag tag me as a threat? A woman took me aside and searched me, intimately; another security agent took my bag off the X-ray machine and went through its contents carefully and thoroughly.

Once through, I headed for the toilets, seeking a moment of privacy from what I had begun, panicked, to believe was surveillance. I locked myself in a cubicle and sat on the closed toilet seat. For the first time I wondered whether I might not be allowed onto the plane, whether I might not be allowed to return to Israel at all. What if, at the gate, when they searched my hand-luggage, as the woman told me they would do, they were to find the maps, the contact details? What if I had been watched, because of being in contact with Zochrot, and Palestinians, because of going to the West Bank; what if I were questioned more closely? Would I be kept so long that I would miss the flight? I didn't know what to do about the maps, the contact details. Surely it was stupid to be concerned, I thought, trying to calm my racing heart. I was not important. I was not doing anything dangerous. I was not in contact with anyone dangerous. But how did I know that? How could I be sure? There was a simple, legitimate answer to any question about the maps if they were to find them, but it would lead to other questions. The questioning might go on, in different forms, for hours – or I might be left for hours, waiting, while they consulted, or forgot, or just for the hell of it, and I would miss my flight. Not because of the maps themselves, or the contacts – but because they would know I had been lying, that I was in fact hiding something, guilty; that I was, in both senses of the word, suspicious.

Reluctantly, I crumpled up the maps and tore out the incriminating pages of my notebook and put them in the bin for sanitary towels. I would be able to retrieve everything I needed later, from email. I could get new maps where I'd got these ones, at Zochrot, in Tel Aviv.

By now I had no desire to go to Israel. Part of me, perversely, wanted to be refused entry – so that my ambivalent, conflicted relationship with the place would be decided for me: so that I could be done with it.

At the gate, the other passengers looked at me with coldness as we waited to board. When I got to the head of the queue, I was taken behind a screen, where another agent examined each item in my hand-luggage and scanned it for explosives. She opened and leafed through every page of my book, my notebook, my document wallet. She would have found the maps.

At that moment I hated them, security agents and passengers alike. I resented their easy identity, their untroubled beings, their claim on Jewish legitimacy. The last time I had travelled to Israel, I could so easily have been recruited. I had been vulnerable. I had lost my sense of the past, my sense of place. I'd wanted to fall in love again with something, with someone – but it was only lonely cab drivers who offered themselves to me, and the moment had passed. How different it felt now, going back: not anticipation and excitement, but hostility, guilt and suspicion, mine and theirs. In my hurt, in my sense of rejection, I had never hated the ugly crudity of Israel more. It seemed so clumsy, what these security agents had done, and done so publicly: what better way to reinforce what you're suspicious of and threatened by than such crude, isolating, demeaning mistrust? Yet was I not guilty of exactly such a mistrust myself? Mistrusted, watched, repeatedly questioned, I myself became hostile and detached, myself a watcher.

The rabbis failed in their efforts, blowing their shofars at 30,000 feet, to keep swine flu out, and in Tel Aviv I succumbed. I had never felt so ill, so feeble. My aunt Myriam thought it might be swine flu, but I *knew* it was swine flu. In my fever, particularly at night, the prospect of travelling to Jordan took on obsessive, delirious nightmare qualities. I followed elaborate, anxious fantasies about the bus breaking down in the desert, about spending hours

dehydrated at the border, getting lost in dangerous neighbourhoods where there were no women in the street; about
not being allowed back in to Israel if I crossed from Jordan
to the West Bank (there were rumours about border guards
giving entry permission restricted to the West Bank). I
dwelled, fearful, on what would happen if I inadvertently
caused offence, if I got food poisoning... At its worst, when
I woke rasping and dry from the air conditioning, or lay
awake listening to a vindictive, invisible mosquito, my
anxiety focused on the image of filthy, stinking squat toilets,
and on the terrible possibility that I might be offered
sheep's eyes to eat, a Jordanian delicacy reserved for guests.

But Malik didn't call or write; there were no answers to
my emails, or texts, or phone messages asking him when it
would be convenient to meet. Lines from a Shalom Hanoch
song in the 1980s echoed in my head in a feverish refrain –
*Mashiach lo ba; mashiach gam lo metalphen*: 'Messiah's not
coming; the Messiah's not going to phone either.'

At last the grip of flu receded. I could hear again, and
talk, though my throat felt torn. Myriam thought Malik
wouldn't get in touch. She didn't want me to go to Amman.
'Maybe his future wife has objected,' she said. 'You don't
know. They're different from us.'

Still weak, slow, I walked long hours through Tel Aviv,
visiting old neighbourhoods, getting lost. Seeing beggars,
the abandoned hulk of the old central bus station, even the
museum dedicated to the Irgun, one of the early Jewish
terrorist groups, filled me with a renewed nostalgia for a
simple past. I wondered what I really wanted from Malik
anyway. What did I want to ask him, and why? Was it simply
his living reality, the fact of his existence that might make
the present clearer in some way, or was it in order to feel
better about myself?

I mistrusted my motives, mistrusted myself, and somehow I communicated this, because I was not trusted anywhere. When I flew south to Eilat, from the tiny domestic airport north of the Tel Aviv port, I was once again under surveillance. Again two different security agents interrogated me at length. Again my passport was taken away to be checked. When I asked why, the second agent said, 'What, you've never travelled in Israel before? You've never been through security?' *Yes,* I wanted to say, I have, *but it's never been anything like this.* The repeat of the interrogation was suggestive and worrying. Why was I being targeted? Because of contact with a political cousin? Because I had published an anxiously critical article or two in a cultural magazine, or because I'd signed up, briefly, with a Jewish peace group? Was my name on some list?

The interrogation over, I was allowed to board, and I sat shakily in the end-seat of the small plane, facing the rear. Opposite me sat a reddened American in his fifties who was travelling to Eilat in order to cross the border to Aqaba and from there travel to Petra to investigate the death of someone, perhaps a relative, in an accident. He and the Israeli with him discussed hotels and taxis and phone calls, and consulted papers and maps in loud voices.

I unwound headphones, set my music player on shuffle, shutting the men's intrusions out, and watched through the scratched window as the dense urban detail of Tel Aviv gave way below us to arid terraced hills, patches of plantations, and agricultural land. The aching voice of Yasmin Levy filled me with her version of the Gypsy lament: '*No tengo lugar, no tengo paisaje, yo menos tengo patria*' – 'I don't have a place, I don't have a landscape, I have a homeland least of all...'

Jerusalem appeared, the Dome of the Rock tiny and

gleaming, and then slipped behind us. We reached the below-sea-level chasm of the Dead Sea, the lowest point on earth, and turned south along the migration route of the Rift Valley towards the Red Sea. As the land moved past slowly below us, exposed and indifferent, scratched with small roads, I leaned my face against the blurred convex window, cupping my hands round my eyes to keep the American from seeing that I was crying. It was only a thread of feeling, Romantic and absurd, that let me think *exile*, that let me think that Levy's Gypsy song of longing was my song of longing. It was only a thread of feeling that tied me to the place through which I was once again intent on tramping in search of roots – with a spade on my shoulder, so that I could dig them up.

The variegated kingfisher blue of the Dead Sea appeared, and Reem Kelani's thrumming raw voice swelled over the harsh, wadi-cracked plateaus of the Jordan mountains rising on the far side from the salt-crusted desert edge: 'The northern wind has changed course... our exile has been long... until we meet... *fi Filasteena* – in Palestine.'

If we have such a yearning for homeland, how can we disparage or discount the same longing in others, I wondered – thinking that I recognised that strength of feeling. How could two thousand years of longing for a notional place in the world carry more meaning than the living memory of a real place?

Down there, below us, Henry Baker Tristram had ridden around the salt marshes, mapping and cataloguing the landscape. There, for him, was the simple taxonomic present, into which he could fit bird specimens like the Dead Sea sparrow, which he 'discovered', and 'obtained' with his rifle – and down there, lined up and jostling on the ruined fortifications of Masada were the untidy grackles with their rusty wings, named in his honour. That seemed something to envy: a naming and an owning; not tenuous, contested, but singular and absolute – and the naivety to believe it innocent.

Gilad Atzmon's lamenting saxophone cut in, and I remembered the long, slow opening shot of the French film *Mur* over which this song now plays: heavy slot after heavy slot of the high concrete separation wall coming down, swaying slightly, tortuously slow, to cut off the vista of the West Bank village beyond it. I remembered interviewing Atzmon in his London flat, his intense blue eyes and maniacal laugh. I'd met him after he'd had a public spat with the Board of Deputies of British Jews over an alleged attempt to boycott a concert of his, because of his anti-Israel views. Seeing his familiar body language, his gestures, and hearing his accent, I thought – though didn't say – how he was still an Israeli despite his repudiation of the very idea of Israel, his repudiation of all forms of Jewish identity beyond a religious one. I wondered if it was precisely because he had grown up in Israel, protected from the direct experience of antisemitism, that he could not understood the resonances of his most extreme statements. I could not in the end find a path through them; I could not find a way to frame and publish the interview.

'Ma'am? *Ma'am*?' the American said loudly, leaning over and touching my knee. I looked round, and removed my headphones. The flight attendant was offering drinks and snacks. I shook my head.

The American asked, 'Are you OK?'

'Yes, I'm fine, thanks,' I said, turning back to the window.

He looked out of his. 'It's beautiful, isn't it?' he said.

'Stunning,' I replied.

Enough to make you weep.

Eilat is baked hard in unremitting late summer heat. The view from my aunt's apartment is of the Red Sea gulf and the desert mountains, harsh and purple. They sharpen against the deepening orange of the hot evening horizon. After dark the heat continues unchanged as though the sun has not set, and in the morning, stepping out into sunlight is like walking into something solid.

Still waiting to hear back from Malik, I take my binoculars and go out birdwatching, as I did here when I was a child. Once Malik gets in touch I can take a taxi to the border crossing, and then, on the other side, a bus from Aqaba to Amman.

A little way down the street from the apartment building, three bicoloured crows are picking at something shrivelled and black at the base of a carob tree. The fallen pods rustle and crackle under their feet. This is the new alien resident. In Tel Aviv it is mynahs and ring-necked parakeets, but in Eilat it is the house crow, an Indian bird that stowed away on container ships and is spreading from the subcontinent to a widening scatter of ports. From the Red Sea it has begun to make its first appearances in Europe, establishing small breeding colonies in Holland and Portugal. An 'invasive species' – but unlike the parakeets and mynahs, and like the settling Jews here in the nineteenth century, the early years of the twentieth, not yet a problem, not yet claiming contested resources, not yet displacing others.

The three dark birds are curious, and look up at me as I pass, with that inimitable crow knowingness. Unafraid, they step to the side at the last possible moment. There's something very Jewish about the crow family – or, to be more precise, something about them that fits ancient stereotypes about Jews: adaptable, clever, good at languages, and they too accumulate wealth, collecting anything shiny; they too suffer from a love of glitz and kitsch. It's so tempting, so easy, to see birds here in human terms. It's impossible not to think about the language with which bird behaviour and belonging is described, and compare it to the truths and omissions in the description of variants of human belonging – 'invasive' or 'indigenous', 'migrant' or 'resident'...

Down on the seafront, past the last hotel and out where the drainage canal empties into the tip of the Red Sea by the Jordanian border, the beaches are reef gravel – small moulded bits of dead coral rounded and smoothed from its spiky hardness, mixed with sand and stone, and fragments of shell. Swimming, this close to the border, is forbidden, and away from the beach hotels there are no toilets or bars or music; there are no lounge chairs for hire for six shekels, or ice-cream, or espresso outlets. It's just the bare expanse of the beach with a single outside shower unit, a van selling water, beer and snack food, and an open, palm-roofed structure providing a little shade.

The paved road becomes a sandy track, and a rusted yellow sign warns, 'Border area ahead: entry forbidden'. Where the canal drains into the sea, an egret is picking its way, dainty and careful, hesitating each step with one yellow foot raised, along the edge of the garish green-blue water. The canal is edged with dark weed and a scum of rubbish and plastic bottles; the water is piped under the track and spills into a holding pan before leaking out to the sea. It is part treated sewage, part fresh water, and a bird haven.

It's already eleven o'clock and 35 degrees, and I am not really prepared for birdwatching, because I'm wearing a loose, light-coloured dress that flaps in the desert wind – and as I cross to the other side of the track, a large heron shifts suddenly from its watch for fish into a tense alert watch of me. There are sentinel herons hunched all along the canal, spaced at intervals, five or six of them, and each of them stretches up suddenly, and takes one or two nervous steps away upstream. A spur-winged plover flies off, calling, with the same clipped wingbeats as a peewit. I remember the first time I saw one, at the edge of the Ruler Road, when we drove to the kibbutz in 1978, my sharp excitement over its instantly identifiable black and white patterning, which I knew from the birdbook. Something of that childhood excitement squeezes me, seeing it again now.

The herons watch me, poised, and the only movement is my dress whipping against my legs and a distant jeep creeping silently along the border road beyond the canal. Then three spur-winged plovers shift out of their freeze, and begin again to make repeated little anxious calls, dipping and shivering slightly each time; the herons relax from their stretched posture, and hunch back into their watch for fish. There are a lot of fish; they keep roiling and breaking the surface of the water.

When it rains, in the winter, the sandy desert soil clumps into a sticky lumpy mud, which dries into a crust. My feet break through the hardened surface as I walk off the track and along the canal. I scare a brilliant turquoise Eurasian kingfisher, which flashes upstream. Behind a pile of newly dug soil, someone has left jeans and a shirt, tyre tracks and hoof-prints. Beyond the canal lie the fences and detritus and dilapidated buildings and boats of the border. The crossing itself lies a few kilometres to the north, and here there are only weathered military watchtowers and tattered flags. Someone has crossed here, or swum ashore at night, and has been met.

I look at the herons through binoculars, hoping for a smaller, scarcer purple heron among the common familiar greys, and then, birdwatching providing cover for a more suspect act, I turn to look across the border at Aqaba, a resort town like Eilat – but not like Eilat.

This is the point where you can see four states: Jordan, Israel, Egypt and Saudi Arabia – or at least you can imagine you see Saudi Arabia in the southern haze. The proximity with Jordan sends a prickling little thrill of adrenaline through me. As a child and a teenager, all the borders seemed absolute – this long eastern one; the southern border with Egypt, at that time much further south in the Sinai Desert; and the northern borders with Lebanon and Syria. There was no possibility of crossing them then: their barbed wire, minefields and warning signs marked the dangerous boundary of the forbidden. It gives me a kind of illicit pleasure: here it begins, *difference*; here this territory instead of that; here this is permitted instead of that; here this language ends and that one begins. I am drawn to the border, to all borders: to watchtowers and barbed wire and machine guns; to arbitrary certainties – *here and no further*.

The pleasure of identifying birds is something similar, I think – not so much the impetus to name and own (or to shoot and name and own, like Tristram), but to distinguish what is known from what is not known, to experience crisp, sharp certainty. But it's also the pleasure of looking, of watching and observing – a voyeurism we don't permit ourselves elsewhere. And how we watch! With binoculars and telescopes and twenty-four-hour webcams – with all the paraphernalia of surveillance. This particular species in its snowy plumage, for example, with its slim red bill, paddling pretty coral-coloured feet in the poisonous green water? It's a slender-billed gull. The egret is a little egret. I put up the herons – suddenly they take off, first one, then all, in a rising progression along the canal. In that light, as they heave their heavy wings, heading over me towards the lagoon, they seem huge, like vultures.

I look over at Aqaba, on the far side of the border, its ridiculous enormous flagpole with the oversized Jordanian flag flying against the bare mountains. I could go to Amman without waiting to hear from Malik. I could take a cab to the border crossing, and then a cab to Aqaba, and there get on the bus to Amman. Once in Amman I could call Malik to ask if we could meet and talk over coffee. It would be easy enough. I could go at a moment's notice, even though Ramadan is about to begin. But I don't go. I wait for Malik, and he doesn't phone, or write.

That evening, I walk up the hill to go in search of sandgrouse, which come in from the desert at dusk each day and stop to drink at the pumping station just beyond the edge of the city. The sun, dropping behind the Eilat mountains, still blazes opposite on the Jordanian mountains, on the far side of the rift in which the Red Sea trickles to its end. Down in the dark flatlands, Eilat and Aqaba spring into a gleam of strung lights around the bay, but the tops of the mountains, harsh, bare and cracked, are lit purple in the last of the sun above the dark valley. The desert light tears at me. I think people might go mad with a wild love for this place, living here.

High up, at the edge of the city, you walk past the last building and suddenly you're in the desert. There's only the road that circles to the west of Eilat and off through the Negev towards Gaza. The boundary between city and desert is unexpected, and final. It is an extreme place – not extreme like the heaving, angry human density of Tel Aviv or Jerusalem, but an extreme environment: the city is there on sufferance. Seen from beyond its border, it looks like a presumptuousness, a human delusion of permanence bounded by an implacable landscape.

Now that the sun is lower and I am high up, it is not as hot, though the wind still blows like an open fan oven. I cross the last road, raising dust clouds from the sandy pink soil, and walk up the track into wilderness. The low scrubby trees, some kind of tangled tarabinth, seem almost dead, but I can imagine what will happen when the rain eventually comes. I can't identify the scattered, low ground-cover. If my uncle David were alive, I would call him up and ask him; I would bring him samples. If I were to ask my mother, she would say, self-deprecating, 'Well I'm not sure what the *real* name is, but we always called it...' That's what I want: to know the names of plants through growing up with them, among them, as I did in England; to know them instantly as I know beech or birch or oak, broom and gorse, cowslips and harebells. I want to have been enculturated, like her, by my grandfather, who travelled all over Palestine collecting plants for the garden he made out of the kibbutz. In this cross-roads of three deserts – the Negev, the Arava and the Sinai – the low wind-blown desert shrubs are particular, perhaps occurring only here, but I have no idea what they are. I have that sense everywhere in Israel, now – that I am always missing something, some information or knowledge, no matter how carefully I look.

Beyond the curve of rock, out of sight of city and road, I am suddenly alone in the desert, and there is only the wind sounding among the rocks and through the wadi, and the electrical jarring of the pumping station, supplying water to the city.

When my father heard I was going to Eilat, he remembered that there had been a leaking tap near my aunt's apartment, where namaqua doves came down at night to drink. 'I don't suppose... Well, I shouldn't think it would still be there,' he said on the phone. There is no longer a tap leaking under the apartment building: water is a valuable commodity, and neglecting its conservation is a social taboo. Wasting water is dangerous in a country depending on diminishing rivers, depleted aquifers and brief rain-fall. All of it is reused. The Jordan river is drying up, much of it diverted for agriculture and other human use, and the level of the Dead Sea, which it feeds, drops metre by metre. There are controversial plans to open a channel from its southern point to the Red Sea, plans to feed desalinated water from the Red Sea back into this landlocked salt lake.

In the West Bank, water is trucked in to Palestinian villages; it is poor quality, inadequately treated and in-adequately stored, and in some areas there are reports of endemic diarrhoea among children. The Jewish settlements, refreshed by blue, chlorinated swimming pools, discharge untreated sewage that contaminates land and seasonal waterways.

Some believe that it will not in the end be land, or borders, or holy places and settlements, but water that will decide things here. With diminishing water resources, what will Israel trade for it, in the end? What might Israel be compelled to trade for water in the end?

A few moments after I sit down on a rock near the pumping station, the birds that have been keeping still, and watching, reappear. A pearl-grey blackstart springs up and away and lands, cocking its dark tail. Palm doves are lining up to roost. A pair of southern grey shrikes settles, too. Among a tangle of dense, fine branches, two small birds begin to chase one another, closer and closer to me, flying from scrubby tree to scrubby tree. They are sunbirds. These are the only sunbirds I have seen in all the time I've been here: this visit, the previous visit. It has been twenty years since I've seen the green iridescence of the Palestine sunbird, which, when I was a child, we called the orange-tufted sunbird.

I wait until dark but the sandgrouse don't come. When I walk back down the track, the cities spread out around the bay are brilliant and glowing, and in the harsh desert landscape all that human effort seem just a little scratch of temporary light.


Birdwatching is a strange pastime. This place is one of the world's most important bird migration corridors. More than five hundred species follow this flight path between Africa and Europe and in total some half a million birds pass through Eilat twice a year. Though autumn migratory birds have started to arrive, it's still too early in the season for the mass of birdwatching tourists with their surveillance equipment, and I'm glad to be able to go birdwatching alone. I don't like birdwatchers, not the dedicated ones. I cringe away from their pointing expertise, their specialist equipment and clothes, their beards and life-lists and pockets, and fussy vocabulary of the 'tick' and the 'drop'. Birdwatchers are predominantly male, and they can be competitive and obsessive. Many of them, in camouflage and kit, are playing at soldiers. If they could, some of them would still be using guns rather than binoculars to collect new specimens for their lists. For others there is a distasteful element of ownership and desire for control in their birdwatching – and of ownership and control of the drab wives who trail along beside them. The women are told where to look, are informed about what they are seeing; their hesitant suggestions of identification are dismissed.

Even my father, a gentle, careful man, becomes authoritarian with a pair of binoculars in his hands.

It's also not yet far enough into the migration season for the bird-ringing station north of Eilat to be open, and so I have the place to myself when my aunt drops me there the next day on her way to work. A group of squacco herons takes off in a noisy flapping panic from the treetops at my approach, and from the hide overlooking a small lake I see grey herons, egrets, black-winged stilts. Some birds I know instantly – the plovers, and the black-winged stilts that I saw first as a child at the edge of the kibbutz's shallow sewage ponds, where the effluent was treated by sunlight and reused for irrigation. There's a long-dormant bird knowledge waking up in me, and an almost physical pleasure in this instant identification. Perhaps after all my delight in birds is not so different from that of the 'real' birdwatcher – this desire to watch and know, this naming and owning.

The look-out place over the salt evaporation ponds has bird identification boards, and a memorial to soldiers who died in the war in Gaza. Among the distant waders at the edge of the ponds, I make out a redshank and a ringed plover. Far off beyond the salt works and the palm groves, the beach-front hotels waver in the growing heat. I think it might be a couple of miles away, and I decide to walk it rather than catch a cab back to the city from the border crossing.

As I come out in the open under the hot sky, a bee-eater takes off and flies up towards the sun. It hangs there, spread and displayed as though it were a small soaring hawk, its green and blue plumage and gold, red and black markings sharply defined in the morning light. I stop every few moments to look. The scrub, and then the palm grove, and then the open bit of desert is alive with birds along a seep of water towards the Red Sea. Under the palms it is red-backed and lesser grey shrikes, masked like small film-noir gangsters. Along the margins of the water slick there are wheatears: common wheatears, desert wheatears, and Isabelline wheatears – they are there all the time as a slight flicker of movement out of the corner of my eye. The bee-eater keeps company above me, its pointed wings spread in brilliant colour. And suddenly, with a jarring interruption of that quiet stillness, my phone rings.

It is my mother, calling from Australia to ask where I am, what I'm doing. As always when I come back to Israel, my uncle and aunts have enquired about her, have given me messages for her, have wanted to know when she is coming to visit; they regret that she doesn't call, that she rarely writes. I want to tempt her back. I want to hear that it hurts her, this place, just a little. But no enquiries after her, no message of love from her sisters or brother, no family story will tempt my mother to come back – she has moved too far away in feeling and in time, so instead I tell her about the bee-eater above me, about the shrikes, the wheatears and spur-winged plovers, and about the spread of house crows. The birds of her past pull at her: I can hear that slightly tender, falling note of nostalgia in her voice after I describe them.

More than anything, I want what I have been pursuing, digging around in matters that are private and past, to break through to her, to break in to her locked-up private space of emotion. But apart from that first time I spoke to her in Hebrew, the note of nostalgia is all she ever allows me to see of what was once a powerful homesickness. Perhaps it is all she can allow herself, or perhaps she does not feel it anymore. Maybe it is only my imagination or need that makes me think she ever did.

Beyond the palm plantation, the muezzin broadcasts the

call to prayer, just the other side of the border – that border I have feared crossing, and which now, it seems, hearing nothing from Malik, I will not cross. I walk for two hours, and by the time I come out of the desert at the edge of the city, I am light-headed with heat and hunger and the shimmering landscape, and my legs are white up to the knee with dust.

At the boundary of the city, before I cross the bridge over the spit of the lagoon to the first hotel, a young man on a moped speeds towards me along the empty road and stops. He asks me, in Hebrew, what time it is. I check and tell him, and hearing my accent he switches to English. 'Where you have come from?' he says. 'Did you just come from *Jordan*? From the border?'

I remember seeing an army jeep moving along the track on the far side of the canal, both this time and the day before. There are almost no soldiers visible in Eilat, almost no border guards or police. It is a holiday resort, after all, a place where Israeli Jews come to forget, to escape the constant reminders of insecurity, and where tourists manage to stay in ignorance of any threat. But the soldiers and border guards are there, out of sight, and I have been under surveillance: I've been observed, and tracked, and reported.

'I've come from the bird place,' I say.

'The beard place?' he repeats, puzzled.

'*Tziporim*,' I explain.

'Ah, *birds!*' he says, and turns round and drives back over the bridge into the city. My odd behaviour has fallen into a recognisable, tolerated pattern. Birdwatching accounts for the direction I've walked, the dust, the staggering dehydration and the expression of slight desperation. And it is true in another more personal way too, perhaps. Perhaps, after all, birdwatching explains a great deal about me, about why I am here, and why I keep coming back.

At airport security in Eilat, heading north, I am interrogated again and disbelieved, and I become sick of it all – sick of waiting to hear from Malik, of paying attention, and above all sickened by Israel and its brutality, and now its sustained mistrust. I am not going to meet Malik; I am not going to be transformed by his story into some kind of clarity, or certainty. I am not sure I even care about him or his story anymore.

This time when I reach the Jezreel Valley, everything is familiar, tugging at me, and yet everything has changed. The bus passes boys selling watermelons by the road, skirts Mount Gilboa, and settles into the straight stretch past the fishponds. Then it slows to a stop beyond the mass of Shatta prison. The prison and the landscape are no longer trembling with my uncertainty, suggesting the presence all the time underneath of another untold or unknown history. It isn't duality or contradiction now, so much as complexity, and I am tired of that complexity. I want it to be simple again. I want to be finished with the past, and with its stories. I want to go back to where I started, at the age of ten. But of course it wasn't simple when I was a child, either; then it was my mother who became complex, and I hated Israel too.

Now the trilingual green metal sign to the kibbutz pulls at me, with its arrow straight on to Beit She'an, and its left arrow to Beit Hashita. I get off the bus and cross the road to walk up to the kibbutz. Everywhere, there are birds. Now that I am looking once again, they have come back into focus, sharply into focus against that heavy, complex landscape. Under the avenue of eucalyptus trees enclosing the road up to the gate, two striped hoopoes are digging in the ground with their beaks open, crests cocked. They swagger like crows. Hoopoes are dirty birds, somehow: they are unkosher, perhaps because they foul their nests, or are omnivores. Even so, they took precedence over the problematically named Palestine sunbird as the representative bird of Israel in the sixty-year anniversary celebrations of 2008. They are cocky and vulgar, rejecting bourgeois manners and embracing peasant earthiness, like my old idea of kibbutzniks.

It is near midday, and here too there is a hot wind, but when a kibbutznik slows to offer me a lift, I shake my head. I don't want to say who or what I am; I don't want to explain about my mother, to carry greetings to her from a distant schoolfriend, to explain where she is living, and why she doesn't come back.

A little further on there is a rustle in the brittle blades of fallen eucalyptus leaves by the side of the road, and a long grey-brown animal with a whiskered face a little like an otter slips across an open patch of ground. It's a porcupine, the first porcupine I have ever seen. Despite my breathlessness in the hot and dusty wind, I am glad I walked.

Asaf's wife Chaya is between shifts when I arrive at their house. She is unchanged, and laughs when I tell her so. Later, when Asaf gets home from the factory, he asks, 'So, what do you want to do while you're here?'

Last time he took me to meet Abu Omar, and we drove past the site of Al Murassas. I think about the ruined villages, and I think about migrating birds. 'I want to see birds,' I tell him. 'I'd like to go birdwatching. Might you be interested in going up to the Huleh valley?'

'Of course, we can do that,' he says. There is a pause.

'That's all?'

'That's all.'

He looks puzzled, uncertain, and then a little relieved.

The next day we drive north-east towards the Galilee and then north towards the Golan. The Huleh valley was once a swamp, and is now fertile agricultural land, but there's a network of protected ponds and canals, where, as at Eilat, migrant birds stop and rest in their thousands. Once we leave the information centre, everywhere we look there are clouds of large orange butterflies, their wingtips barred with white and black. They cluster in fluttering masses. It is a butterfly migration, like the monarch migration you can sometimes see in California, only these are African monarchs on their way south for the winter.

Overhead, far above, floats a skein of large birds. The Huleh is famous for its crane migration, and I look at them in hope, but it is too early for the cranes. These are storks. The white egrets, lined up on the long field irrigators with their necks hunched back into their shoulders, look sullen and irritated as around them and around us, in ones and twos, the storks begin to descend, circling round and down into the field, their red legs dangling.

At the bird hide we run into Itzik: he is the half-brother of my half-aunt-in-law's sister's husband. This makes him family. He works as a warden of the bird reserve. 'How are you? What are you up to these days?' he says, as though we have known one another for a long time. Last time we met, years before, we talked a little about birds, a lot about family.

'All she has in her head is birds,' says Asaf, looking delighted. '*Nothing* in her head but birds.'

'Excellent!' says Itzik. 'That's all she *should* have in her head.'

He points across the open water before us, naming what

is visible that morning: to the right, a group of spoonbills, black-tailed godwits and ruffs. A cluster of glossy ibises are keeping themselves separate. There are grey herons everywhere – migrating herons, Itzik says, and to the left, a small flock of white pelicans.

'Herons migrate?' I say. 'I had no idea.' I think of the herons along the irrigation canal in Eilat, and of the herons I see hunched by the river and in the fields at home in Wales.

'Yes, yes – they migrate,' Itzik says. 'And they roost together, in big groups, in the trees. Not like the pelicans. Pelicans roost together and feed together, but herons roost together and then they separate to feed.'

'Very sensible,' I say.

'I prefer the pelicans' way,' he says, 'eating together, too – but then, I'm still a socialist, a real kibbutznik.' He looks at Asaf and they both laugh.

Itzik's kibbutz is still a traditional socialist collective, but a century on from the earliest communist foundations of the movement, many kibbutzim have changed course. Beit Hashita is no longer under the illusion that it's self-sufficient. It no longer even owns its own land. In the aftermath of the Israeli financial crisis of the mid-1980s, when the currency was devalued and the manageable debts that most kibbutzim carried became suddenly crippling, Beit Hashita also suffered, and Ossem, an Israeli company, bought the canning factory; in turn Ossem was bought by Nestlé. Asaf has lived all his life in a community that operated on the socialist principle of each giving what he could, and each having what he needed, and until the kibbutz sold off its assets he was a worker in a factory owned by workers. Now as the factory logistics manager, he's the employee of a global multinational.

Caught out, a little ashamed, I want to agree with Itzik, to say that yes, he is of course right about the pelicans' social-ism. I hadn't thought about bird behaviour in those terms. Here in Itzik is the unreconstructed kibbutznik, the idealist, and a little flame of rekindled kibbutz romanticism leaps up in me, despite what I know now about the kibbutz movement's contradictions and hypocrisies and denials, despite what I know about Shatta – and about all the other Shattas, before and after 1948. A longing for innocence closes over me, and I turn to look out at the pelicans to cover up my reaction.

Itzik asks what I've seen in Eilat, what we've seen so far in the Huleh, and briskly I become a twitcher, ticking, for Eilat, *redshank, little plover, squacco heron, slender-billed gull, Caspian tern, sunbird, redbacked shrike, southern grey shrike, bee-eater, common wheatear, desert wheatear, Isabelline wheatear, blackstart...* and for the Huleh valley, *roller, hoopoe, Smyrna kingfisher, little egret, cattle egret, marsh harrier, purple heron, white stork, avocet, red-rumped swallow...*

But when Asaf and I get back to the information centre and car park, there's one more to add: a masked shrike sitting on a telephone line, like a little final gift. Further along, at safe distance, swallows are sitting in a huddle, watching him uneasily. I know him in the instant of seeing him, though I've never seen a masked shrike before – that odd immediate bird certainty that feels like a deep and absolute knowledge rather than identification arrived at by some process of comparison and exclusion.

Perhaps such simple certainty was what birdwatching offered to my parents when we visited Israel in 1978 and 1980, when I was ten, and twelve; perhaps this was their way of dealing with all that my mother must have felt leaping up in her, coming home. Everything that pulled at her after fifteen years – her family, her language, her country – must have been evident to my father, too. How could either of them have been able to articulate it, that emotional charge, with all the threat to their settled quiet life in England that it carried? Birds for them might have been a way of coping with complexity, rather than a way of avoiding it.

It's not what I am doing, returning in this way to birds. It's more the case that I'm sick of complexity, exhausted by how it implicates me – and exhausted, too, by the way this routine, impersonal and dehumanising surveillance is accusing me when I have committed no wrong. But it's not just the suspicious authorities, for whom the questioning of the past undermines the state's legitimacy, to whom I feel I have to protest that I am innocent – it's the mistrustful others, too: those for whom my questioning and acknowledgement of guilt doesn't go far enough.

Mistrust and suspicion undermines you; it reduces you. It leaves you scrabbling at the feet of those who have judged you and found you untrustworthy. The more you seek to assure them of your trustworthiness, the more you reinforce their right to judge you. The mistrust of others creates an unease about yourself that you can never quite eradicate – and I want, terribly, to be exonerated, to be free of it. I want to feel again the innocence I had when I was not yet under surveillance, when I had not yet experienced being mistrusted, when I could still look with curiosity at everything, free of the fear that looking made me a voyeur. I want to be ten years old again, back when borders were simple and dangerous, airport security provided safeguards against the PLO, and I had nothing in my head but birds.

# 6 – Claiming dominion

Back at the kibbutz, I lie in the shuttered cool of my cousin's vacant apartment, listening to the fan turn from side to side. Here I am in walking distance of the ruined village that Malik's family is from: Al Murassas and Yubla are just a few kilometres away. Outside, a dove is calling drowsily from a tall palm. Occasionally mopeds sputter along the paths, but much of the noise of tractors and voices is stilled during these hottest hours. It is siesta time, but though I have not slept properly for weeks I cannot settle, I cannot sleep. Itzik, watching the socialist pelicans, has rekindled the old longing in me. This *hiraeth*, this *sehnsucht* – though I'm here in the place I love I cannot bear this love. 'I shall lock the door to my heart and throw the key into the sea,' wrote Rahel, one of the poets of early modern Hebrew. It's a wild and damaged love I have for this place. How can I *not* want this feeling of connection?

I give up the attempt to sleep and make coffee and take it outside. Sitting on the step, I watch a pair of jays on the dry grass, catch a fleeting metallic glint of a sunbird. Two bulbuls are fluttering in the dusty shrubs, and there's a smell of eucalyptus and sap. Over it all a scent of incense wafts down from the upstairs flat, where a neighbour, an older man, is listening to sitar music, which floats over the deep thrum and rattle of air-conditioning from the nearby central dining room.

The central dining room, the huge building with cavernous kitchens that dominates every kibbutz, is no longer the communal heart it was when I was a child. Meetings, events, plays, festivals – people still gather for these, but the communal meals are long since gone. Years earlier, when families began to eat alone at home, when children started to spend the night with their parents, those who resisted change warned that this was the beginning of the end. Long after individual homes had ceased to be single bare rooms and became instead self-contained apartments and houses, an adult's home was still euphemistically referred to as a 'room'. Even the earliest changes – personal possessions, a kettle in the 'room' – were seen as a serious threat to the shared communal ethos of the kibbutz, and the advent of private showers was believed by some to be a bourgeois indulgence that would destroy the community.

Everyone now eats at home. Young people used to leave for army service and then go on to found new kibbutzim or to support and reinforce struggling border settlements. Now in the absence of a bond made from necessity and survival, of hardship and unity against attack, an ideal (if not always an actuality) of labour in service of the collective, the children, untempered by those rigid communal structures, grow up without a collective ideology. Without gravity pulling them in, they spin off, out of orbit, and don't come back. When my mother abandoned kibbutz life altogether in the 1960s it was an anomaly, but now it is common. My mother's sister left Beit Hashita, too; two of Asaf's children also moved away when they reached adulthood, though all of them have continued to live on other kibbutzim. Young people go away for the army, for university, and keep moving. The high school closed, and the kindergarten shrank. Of my family, only Asaf remains, with his wife Chaya, and my cousin Amit. Asaf and Chaya had their doubts too, their crisis, but they have stayed. It's changing again, now. A new neighbourhood is being built, and a new kindergarten has opened, but the people who move to the kibbutz do not become members; now it is more like a village than a kibbutz.

Behind me, through the open door, I can hear the old fridge rattling. Asaf or Chaya stocked it for me; they've left cheese, bread, jam and cake, and juice and bottled water. On the counter stands a jar of sugar and the new tin of Elite instant coffee that I have just opened. It makes me ridiculously nostalgic. The first coffee I ever drank was iced coffee made with powdered Elite by my step-grandmother, when I was thirteen and staying on the kibbutz without my parents for the first time. I thought it was a terribly grown-up thing to drink coffee. In everything that I did and saw at the time lay the coiled excitement of being on the edge of something, on the edge of change – everything was sharpened by the vibrant hot, live beginning of adolescence, when you feel things in extremes, and fall in love for the first time, passionately and absolutely, with a person, or an idea, or a place.

The pale jays strut on the grass, moustached, black-crested. Unlike British jays, which head off lumpily into woodland at any hint of motion or noise, these are unafraid and loud – but they are the same species, that dark cinnamon-coloured crow and this light, creamy Middle Eastern variant. There is a smell of hot dust and resin and eucalyptus, and I am ten again, balancing on that wall outside the central dining room with my sister, noting *bulbul* and *sunbird* and *hoopoe*.

The sitar music swells as the door opens, and my neighbour comes down the stairs to greet me. He sits on the higher step, and offers me a joint. He's wearing a loose purple cotton shirt and smells of patchouli – a soulful man who meditates and does yoga, a spiritual Israeli by way of India and California. He repudiates the stereotype of the macho, brusque, rude Israeli, the dark, tender, wounded Israeli man I made a fetish of when I was twelve and thirteen. His voice is gentle and quiet. He is stoned and laid back, and he reminds me of Nadav, one of the Israeli exiles I met in California, years ago, when I lived there – scarred, gentle sitar-playing Nadav, with thick glasses and delicate hands, who went AWOL, who outstayed his visa, who, like my mother, is never coming back to Israel.

During the night, berries fall continuously from the tree just outside the window, rustling in the dry leaves and undergrowth, and in the morning palm doves begin again softly, a moped speeds along the path by the dining room, car engines start near and far. It is the beginning of a work-day, but nothing like the old dawn noise of the kibbutz, when most of the people who lived here also worked here. I pick up my binoculars, camera, and a bottle of water and walk up through acacias and thick flowering bougainvillea, and the tall date palms that my grandfather planted some seventy years ago. In the 1930s, with characteristic chutz-pah, he stole the saplings off the back of a Jordanian truck. For many years he was the kibbutz gardener, planting it with native species, and adding small signs with the Hebrew botanical names, educating the new community about the valley's familiar but unidentified natural history. During long walks through the valley and the hills to the north of the kibbutz and on Gilboa he lifted bamboos and lilies, sometimes without the owners' knowledge, and brought them back to plant in the kibbutz. Everywhere I look around the kibbutz there are stories of my grandfather. In 1972 he was injured by a drunken English volunteer, and his already poor eyesight was badly affected. After that he concentrated on transforming the cemetery, landscaping it and planting it, so that it has become a park.

I reach the dusty track that leads past the cemetery and the building site of the new neighbourhood, and out over the borderless cultivated fields towards what is left of Al Murassas, towards what is left of Yubla – a road that ends at the visible ruins of Belvoir, the invisible ruins of Kawkab al Hawa.

A pipe is being laid to the new residential neighbourhood of the kibbutz, and tractors and diggers have cut a quarry out of the slope. About half a kilometre's walk from Beit Hashita the road splits. To the left it leads to the Arab villages of Taibe and Na'ura, to Abu Omar and his beautiful grandson. Straight on it leads, in the distance, to the cow pasture and sabra that mark the site of Al Murassas. At the split in the road there's a lookout point, with signage and shade and benches. One sign, a panorama of the landscape, is so sun-bleached that its features are barely distinguishable, but its Hebrew place names, re-inked in permanent marker, stand out darkly: *Kochav haYarden, Tel Yosef, Gilboa...* Newer signs have been put up to mark the development of the Issachar hiking trail. Some are bilingual, with awkward English translation and spelling mistakes, and odd typographical errors: 'Givat Hamore-Ramot Yissachar Scenic Trail begins on a ridge in the Givat Hamore peaks 517 meters in altitude and continus for 32 kilometers along the barren Ramot Yissachar creasts at an average height of 80 meters to the military industries park and Road. 90 in the Beit She'an Valley...' Most of the area, it claims, is associated with famous biblical events. But then a neat eliding of the past leaps out from the densely packed text: it crosses seamlessly, painlessly, from the biblical era to the 1930s. In modern times the area was reforested 'to redeem the land of Israel for Zionist settlement. Yehoshuah Hankin purchased significant tracts of land here for the Jewish National Fund on which settelments were built.' Those non-Jews who shaped the land between biblical times and twentieth-century Jewish settlement are invisible: they do not exist; they did not ever exist.

To the south lies the bulging mass of Mount Gilboa; fishponds glimmer in the distance – the fishponds of Ein Harod or Tel Yosef, built on the lands of Qumiya, which was depopulated early in 1948. Nearer huddles the dense, low enclosure of Beit Hashita, built on land bought in 1931 in the purchase that depopulated Shatta. I can see the green of the kibbutz cemetery at its edge. Around me, and to the north and east, spread the dark-brown ploughed fields that used to belong to Yubla and Kafra, Al Bireh and Al Murassas, with the sand-pale track winding over them. The whole panorama lies before me, and there is nothing to indicate the Arab villages were ever here.

Salman Abu Sitta's *Atlas of Palestine* shows a different landscape: the names of the villages that were depopulated in 1948, reproduced in Arabic, Hebrew and English; the names of the newer kibbutzim and other Jewish settlements, and the symbols marking the sites of mosques and wells, of important tombs and springs and schools. It was photo-copies from that atlas which, rightly anxious, I crumpled and threw away in the toilet cubicle at Heathrow Airport.

A little further on, a second sign, in Hebrew, memorialises Yos and David, two kibbutzniks from Beit Hashita. They are described as a 'peasant' and a 'metal worker'. From this lookout, dedicated to their memory, it is possible, the sign claims, to see the evidence of 'a belief in the righteousness of the way and adherence to the Zionist ideology that brought about the creation of the beautiful valley'. The signboard's reference is biblical: here lies Kibbutz Beit Hashita, whose name derives from the story of Gideon. And here is that same leap – backwards, this time – from the present to the ancient Jewish past, passing over the existence of Shatta, the village that had retained an Arabic form of the same biblical Hebrew name. And this word for 'peasant' – *felach* – so close to the Arabic *fellah*: did kibbutz Hebrew borrow and subvert the Arabic word, and rehabilitate it? Israeli-Jewish attitudes to the fellahin do not differ enormously from the colonial attitudes still present in the English word 'fellah'. Again I am making half-guesses, feeling my way towards meanings, but when, further on, a signboard names another lookout point after the noble Jewish peasants, I realise it is no wonder that I absorbed a story of the kibbutznik as noble peasant. Here is that story written onto the landscape. And yet this is a vista of fields that have been emptied of workers of the land.

Of course it's a truism to say that naming the landscape is an act of storytelling, and an act of dominion and owner-ship, but it's written into our consciousness – Adam, the first human and the first naturalist, naming and claiming dominion. But even if it's a truism to say that the one in a position to name is the one with power, there's a danger in naming, too. The common folk belief that an individual has a true name which must remain hidden in order to cheat death – or the Other, or the fairies, or the underworld – is still powerfully resonant: naming has magical properties. And when the hero or heroine learns that name, or if the antagonist divulges his true name, the balance of power shifts. Rumpelstiltskin, his name unguessed, cackles and rubs his bony hands together, the image of a stereotyped scheming, chaos-inducing Jew because he is outside, he is *other*, he is mutable and unknowable, his affiliations and his knowledge secret and inaccessible. But naming him by his true name renders him impotent. And the resonance of those folk beliefs is surely connected to an uneasy consciousness of how naming a child has something of this dangerous control about it, too. A baby is part of the generality of babies, unmarked by the first definitions of gender or weight, or the length and nature of the labour, or whether he or she cried at birth. These are impersonal details: none of these is a designation, and your own consciousness of him or her is incomplete, formless. But when you name a child, you stamp down your own classification, your own story; you exclude the possibility of other stories.

My older daughter is named Jericha, a feminised form of the world's most ancient city, Jericho. She was conceived in Jerusalem, but Jerusalem carries within it the consciousness of Jericho, to which it is connected by an ancient trade route, the Jericho Road. The old names, the old routes are still there – Jericho and Jerusalem, Jerusalem and Jaffa, Jerusalem and Nablus. You can orientate yourself in the one city by an awareness of the other. My daughter is named after that ancient city, an imagined city of the moon, her name an evocation of cityscape and palimpsest, of ancient library mazes and mosaic floors, founded on ritual deposits – white-clay masks with haunting shell eyes.

I was thirteen when I first heard about those archaeological finds of masks at Jericho, which, my history teacher Mr Davidson said, was in Jordan. It was 1981, and I had been to Jericho the previous year, had seen the mosaic floor of its recently excavated ancient synagogue.

I put up my hand. 'Excuse me, Mr Davidson,' I said, 'but Jericho's in Israel.'

'No,' he replied, 'it's in Jordan.'

'But I've *been* to Jericho,' I protested, puzzled. 'We went last year, when we were in Israel.'

This was my first encounter with a different version of the past – not the Leon Uris version, not the Israeli one, not the Zionist one. But in that unfamiliar version, the West Bank was still understood, at the time, to be occupied Jordan, and Gaza to be occupied Egypt: the territories had not yet become Occupied Palestine in the popular imagination.

When people puzzle over the source of my daughter's name, I have to explain – because of what Jericho means, what it can mean – that the choice was not a claim of cultural or geographic or historical dominion over ancient Jericho and therefore a political claim on modern Jericho, but an invocation of that imagined city of the moon, emblem of all cities. Naming isn't about identifying; it's about trying to sear a brand into the flesh of a thing, about trying to make something permanent out of the telling of a story, an attempt to reduce chaos, to impose order.

Did my daughter's particular love of cities result from her being named after the world's oldest city? Did we, her parents, unconsciously but not accidentally, write Jericho and Jerusalem into her, seeking to shape her origins in our shared story as much as seeking to determine her future? How you are named determines who you are in fundamental ways, but it is not immutable. If only we could still believe that truth is pure and unchanging, rather than contingent, that chaos is reducible to perfect order, that there are absolute names for things. But everywhere I look I see naming as an act of storytelling that conceals, a process of reshaping and erasing the past in order to determine the future.

On the crest of the hill some three kilometres away, I make out the stand of trees that marks what remains of Al Murassas. I have one small bottle of water, and I am wearing thin sandals that are coming apart, but I set off towards the site of its ruins. Once again the landscape has split into a shimmering multiplicity – the present-day panorama of fertile agricultural land; the remnants in it of another relationship, another past, and the overt signage, with its laboured, over-flowery co-options and omissions, which I did not see from the car when my uncle brought me here the first time to look at cattle and sabra and barbed wire.

Parts of the trail have only recently been landscaped, and here the information boards and boulders with white-lettered inscriptions still look new. The bank has been replanted with pomegranate and oleander, the saplings sheathed in protective plastic that has already been bleached by the sun into a pale discoloured pink.

A flock of larks rises over the bare earth. Perhaps they are early migrating skylarks from Europe. There are no fences here to separate out the crop fields, no boundary markers, just the change from freshly turned soil to crop, to fallow land. The pale track blends on either side into the edges of the field.

My feet begin to hurt. Dusty, sore and thirsty, labouring a little in the heat, I recognise the resonance of a kind of pilgrimage. This isn't a religious pilgrimage, as in Jerusalem, where knots of devout tourists walk, chanting, between the stopping points of the Via Dolorosa, and their guides stand to one side, waiting, while they pay homage or pray; nevertheless, in its own way this is becoming a kind of homage – though I am not sure to what, or to whom.

Ahead of me, in the distance, the site of the destroyed

village is marked out from the fields by a dark line of sabra. As I draw near, I see that the barbed wire is down and the cattle are gone: it is empty, and I can go in.

According to Walid Khalidi, in 1931 Al Murassas was a roughly circular settlement of eighty-nine adobe houses. His figures come from the British 'Census of Palestine' that year. Three hundred and eighty-one people lived here then. By 1945 the population was four hundred and sixty, and in 1948, this had risen to an estimated five hundred and thirty-four. When I read Khalidi's description of Al Murassas to my mother, she said: 'Of course that's not how I remember it. I remember ruins, ruined buildings, bits of walls. Buildings, but not with roofs... We called it *khirbe*. That's what it was.' *Khirbe* means ruins.

'Stone?' I asked. 'Or adobe?'

'Well, I remember stone, but I'm not sure. Maybe that was *beit ha-sheikh*. Or perhaps I'm remembering Kawkab...'

'But you knew, right?'

'Yes, it was the empty villages. We knew they were empty Arab villages.'

I walk down the cattle track from the road and step over the barbed wire lying on the ground. The cattle have eaten everything but the sabra and a low, dry thorny plant that scratches my ankles and penetrates through the worn soles of my sandals. As I come level, like a picture coming into focus, the wild tangle of sabra resolves into a border, a planted boundary hedge. It marks the edge of the village site, and three sides of a square, with a single tree in the centre. The ground is bare except for stubble and thorn and a few scattered rocks. Up on the road, the bank has been built up and landscaped with rock; perhaps it has been taken from ruined houses. Tomer, the kibbutz archivist, remembers the buildings as part stone, part adobe.

From the road I could only see a sabra thicket, but now I see the village itself begin to take shape. I walk a long way through those high sabra boundaries. The site stretches out into enclosure after enclosure, often around a single acacia tree. The cactus hedges are tall, gnarled, scarred and deformed, and impenetrable, like a fairytale thicket. Some of the sabra has broken, and great limbs lie on the ground, but there is new growth, too, and the old growth is still bearing fruit: ripening, and ripe, and fallen.

I enter a corridor of sabra and it is absolutely still; the heat is caught there. On either side of the path, thick cactus grows to some seven or eight feet, shutting out sight of the curve of fields, the rounded hills, the purple and green of Gilboa. I am alone, enclosed in this silent, suffocating avenue of cactus, and it is all I can see – thorned, savage, massive and old. In the pressured hot stillness I can't move: I am caught in this corridor, trapped. The cactus walls lean in, scarred and ancient; they have taken hold of me. Then I am walking again, fast, almost running, in a sudden near panic, until I break out of the corridor and into the open. I scramble away up the slope towards where the road lies, and at a safe distance look back. Behind me, the corridor has become once again only a tangle of cactus.

When Tristram identified Al Murassas among 'several ruined villages' in 1865, perhaps his 'grass-grown sites ... marked afar by a deeper green' were nothing of the sort; perhaps instead they were the darker green of these sabra boundaries, which he saw only from a distance, and about which he made dangerously mistaken assumptions.

Ahead of me a great rusty pipe rises out of the scratchy, dry land, and downhill from it there is a blur of slight green with low shrubs where it leaks a little. Perhaps this is the spring that once rose in Kafra and descended to Al Murassas. A covey of chukars rises at my approach – flight after flight of plump, chestnut-barred partridges taking off from the tiny damp oasis of the leaking pipe in the valley below.

I can see the far edge of the village now, the hedge of sabra marking the boundary, and I follow the pipe up towards the road, where it goes underground. My head is pounding. I have not drunk enough, and there is only an inch of water left in my bottle. Here by the pipe grows the stand of trees that Asaf pointed out the last time, when we stopped. They are in a rough circle – a cypress and a tall eucalyptus rising elegantly to a high canopy, and others I cannot identify. Perhaps this is the site of Sheikh Ibrahim Al Sa'ad's grave, which is marked on Abu Sitta's map, but there is nothing to identify it except the trees. The remains of the rusty pipe protrude here, too. Evidently it has been replaced by a newer high-tech pipe – its junction stands exposed on the far side of the road. Perhaps when this pipe was laid, the Sheikh's bones had to be moved. All construction has to stop, in Israel, when bones are discovered, and the archaeological authorities have to be called in. Jewish religious law forbids the removal of the Jewish dead, so if bones are found, it has to be ascertained that the site isn't one of Jewish burial. Deep history is the bane of Israeli construction companies: wherever you dig there are bones.

I clamber back onto the road. A few feet from the stand of trees, an upright boulder has been placed to mark the hiking trail. It is chiselled with white-lettered Hebrew lines from the poem *Od Chozer ha-Nigun,* 'the melody still returns', by nationalist poet Natan Alterman:

> Still the melody returns which you left behind in vain
> and once again the road opens up along its length
> and a cloud in its sky, and a tree in its rain
> still await you, passer-by.

Knowing what that place once was, the meaning of the poem shifts from the one intended by its being sited there. The melody left behind in vain in that particular place is not the trace notes of a biblical past, referred to elsewhere in the signage, which re-inscribes it in the landscape. Instead it is the lingering melody of a much more recent past, and not trace notes of it, so much as a full lament – the lament of that other map which reads *harus... harus... harus.* Destroyed... destroyed... destroyed...

I walk back along the track, uncomfortably dehydrated. By the time I get within sight of the kibbutz, my head beats with pain, and I am beginning to stagger. My legs are not obeying me and my rings are tight: my hands have swollen. Once back in my cousin's apartment, I kick off my broken sandals, sit down on the bed and gulp glass after glass of cold fruit juice – pear and sabra, with its odd, sweet flavour, and its poignant, sweet and difficult meanings and associations.

When I was ten, we drove along that road, heading for Belvoir up on the bluff that overlooks the Jezreel Valley. My mother was ill at the time, and so the rest of us – my father, brother, sister and I – were going birdwatching without her, in the rented Peugeot 504 that kept overheating. It was April, but in the early morning the interior of the car was already unbreatheable; the *hamsin* was blowing, a hot sandy wind from the desert that made people a little crazed. Before we realised it, we had driven into the midst of butter- flies. My father slowed and then pulled over, and we sat a few moments in the car, watching butterflies in their hundreds. They were not behaving like butterflies as we knew them – fluttering, stopping, making sideways forays from flower to flower, in a random pattern determined by opportunity – but like birds: they were heading somewhere, determined and intent.

We got out of the car. There were butterflies flattened in the balding tyre treads, in the radiator grille, on the windscreen; there were butterflies dead on the road, caught among dry grass stems. They were all painted ladies. Around us and among us and beyond us, through the light and shade of a small stand of cypresses, and all along the slope, they kept coming. We went and looked down the hill and they were rising towards us through the grasses and sabra; we could see the movement a long way off. It is one of my most vivid, sensual childhood memories: the heat, the car's metal smell, the dusty softening tarmac, the butterflies, and my mother somewhere else, ill.

I never knew where it was until, comparing bird memories with my father before travelling again to Israel, I asked where we'd seen the painted ladies. 'At Belvoir,' he said, over the phone. There was a pause. 'Belvoir, the crusader castle. Kawkab al Hawa,' he added. 'I think it means Star of the East.'

The Arabic name means Star of the Winds, not Star of the East. The place is named after the high wind that often blows there – a hot wind, which brings no relief. Until 1948 this was the Arab village of Kawkab al Hawa. In 1948, at that elevation, with a wide view east and south, it offered a strategic military advantage and it was the site of fierce fighting. The village was occupied, depopulated and destroyed by Jewish forces, and nothing of it remains.

The crusader fortress site has long since been excavated and developed as a national park, but although there's no trace of the destroyed village, the park's name retains in its Hebrew version an echo of its older identity, as if in guilty half-acknowledgement – not Kawkab al Hawa, 'Star of the Winds', but Kochav HaYarden, 'Star of the Jordan'.

Despite its official rebranding, despite the deliberate and systematic eradication of the evidence of its physical past, and the rewriting of the landscape under a new name, a fragment of the story of that place persists in memory, too. When I arrived this time at Beit Hashita, Chaya mentioned to me that she and my uncle Asaf had recently been on a little *tiul*, a trip, to Kawkab. Not *Kochav*, the Hebrew name; not Belvoir, the crusader fortress name, but *Kawkab*, the Arabic name. Her uninflected use of the older Arabic name – casual, unacknowledged, unconscious – is mirrored in the name of the Sakhne, too, the hot spring at the foot of Gilboa where I had swum as a child. Sakhne is its Arabic name, though the road-signs to it, and its presence on the map, use the official Hebrew name, Gan HaShlosha. When my mother was a child, the Sakhne was a green splash among rocks; kibbutz children went swimming there with an armed adult standing guard above them. When I was a child, it was an eroded, dusty, littered picnic area full of dangers, with strict segregation between Arabs on the far side and Jews and tourists on the near side.

A road used to lead from Al Sakhina to Al Murassas. Al Sakhina is gone, but the memory of it remains in the name of the spring, the Sakhne. The memory of Al Murassas lives on locally, too, whatever the government intended and attempted, and so does the memory of the other villages.

My uncle knows where they were and what they were. So does his wife Chaya. So does my mother, and Tomer the kibbutz archivist, and the others of their generation. The Arabic names and meanings continue to circulate orally, continue to resonate, identifying features and settlements by the names that the Jewish newcomers learned in the 1920s and 1930s from the Arab residents who were already long settled in the valley. But the official elisions, the transition between ancient history and the present day, are seamless. Inscribed in the landscape in the boards and signposts of the hiking trail, they will become a new truth, and that elided past will be gone from the memory of the next generation. One of my cousins, Asaf's daughter, tells me: 'We learned nothing in school about kibbutz history, about Al Murassas.' She adds, uncertain, 'Is it Al Murassas – is that the name?'

Officially, the places do not exist – and, not existing, can be believed never to have existed – but memory disrupts the official version. They live on in names, in the older generation's sense of place, in images of the landscape from their childhood now changed beyond recognition – my mother's memory of *beit ha-sheikh*; her memory, her generation's memory, of the still-visible ruins of the destroyed villages. They know and don't know – about the destroyed villages and neighbourhoods, the missing three-quarters of a million people, transformed into a threatening, burgeoning five million. They know and don't know because they remember but are required to forget. It is not denial, precisely, so much as silence and omission. And meanwhile, spread through the world in the Palestinian diaspora, the memory of those places is held and cherished in a story handed down through some three generations.

When I talk to him at last, Malik says that there is nothing special about his grandfather's story. He apologises for not having been in touch: he has been very busy with work and preparations for his wedding, and for Ramadan. It is not convenient to meet me in Amman, but we can talk by phone. He says again, 'If you are doing some justified research, I am happy to help your good self.'

It's the day before I leave, and I wonder what I should say to this man, what I now want. *Sorry?* Sorry about your *tsores*, your troubles? Excuse me, but may I have your story for my own purposes, to feel better about myself? Can I harvest your past like some kind of fruit and make a bitter drink out of it? But I ask him anyway – about his grandfather, about what happened, about his own connection to that place now.

Malik's grandfather fled Al Murassas in 1948 and ended up in Irbid, in Jordan, where, except for ten years when he worked in Kuwait, he stayed for the rest of his life. Malik doesn't know enough about it to make it stand out in any way: his grandfather's experience was the same as that of everyone who left. He had been a farmer, and he had to leave his land. Farming was a second income, because mainly his work was as a carpenter, a skilled carpenter. He had worked in Haifa, which was a vibrant city, and he was doing well. When he had to leave, he lost everything. Nevertheless, because he had a skill, he managed well in his new life. He was able to support himself and his family, so he didn't end up living in a refugee camp. He left Palestine with Malik's father, who was about a year old at the time – Malik's grandfather didn't have a birth certificate, but he estimated that he was then about twenty-five – and he never went back, not even to visit. He realised he wouldn't ever be able to return.

I tell Malik I have seen the site of Al Murassas. What must it be like to hear, I wonder, that I can come and go to this place his family is from, that I could, if I wished, take up residence just a few kilometres away.

'This is the place where our roots are; this is where we belong,' Malik says. 'We have rights – we have land and farms. It is our land.' He pauses. 'We know the situation,' he goes on, more emphatically. 'It's harder, now – but we still have a feeling inside that we have rights; that it is our right, this land. It was a tragedy that happened thirty years before I was born; the land was my grandfather's land. He left because of fear – he left everything. You can't blame him.'

It should not surprise me, this hint that there might be shame attached to having fled, but it does. How could members of a younger generation not have blamed the older one for losing them their birthright? And how could the question not be asked whether the Nakba, its tragedy, was something Palestinians might have been able to resist, which was the other side of the popular Zionist claim that they had in part brought it upon themselves?

'If you are doing research,' Malik says, 'that aims to show the truth of the history, I am at your disposal: I am glad to help.'

Truth? What truth, I wonder. That some people fled in fear, that others were driven out – that the creation of more than 720,000 Palestinian refugees was not the result of war but, as Ilan Pappe claims, a deliberate, orchestrated act of ethnic cleansing? The way Pappe presents it, the evidence of systematic ethnic cleansing is not always clear or convincing; stripped of the story he tells about it, that evidence can be subject to different interpretation, but I am no historian, and I don't know any more now about the causes than I did at the beginning – except that there was no single cause, that there is no simple, single historical 'truth'. The two versions are not binary opposites, mutually exclusive narratives, but a confusion of stories, an entangled mass of threads. But one of them is visible in the landscape I have just walked through, and the other has been removed.

I think of that valley, with its newly signposted and landscaped hiking trail, which writes a state-sanctioned story onto a valley that no longer holds the people who once shaped it. Malik's story, and that of others like him, doesn't replace mine. It doesn't stand in for mine. It doesn't in any way moderate my feelings of attachment, though his sense of attachment, of rights, of ownership is just as real, just as strongly felt. But it's my people who are in possession, my people who have dominion; it's my people who inscribe their names and their stories onto the land that once held his people, so it is surely we who are accountable.

When I was nine, my mother came to my school and taught my class the opening of Genesis in Hebrew: 'In the beginning God created the heaven and the earth. And the earth was without form, and void.' I always afterwards loved the expression *tohu v'vohu* – without form, and void – and its King James translation, too. They seemed so different from one another, the Hebrew an almost childish rhyme, but barely there – just a breath and a dissipation – while the English line was so oddly curtailed and abrupt, emphatic. Without form: unidentified, undifferentiated, without name, and therefore void. *Not* naming – not naming the sites of destroyed villages and neighbourhoods, not telling the other story – is a different order of control: *not* naming renders a thing void.

Before our first visit to Israel in 1978, when I used to leaf through my father's precious edition of Tristram's *Fauna and Flora of Palestine,* trying to understand *phylum* and *class, order* and *family, genus* and *species,* trying to memorise relationships and Latin names, it was the tiny iridescent sunbird that I lingered over, the one bird in the book that is found nowhere else in the world. Until Tristram 'obtained' specimens, by shooting them in northern Palestine in the spring of 1864, the sunbird was hardly known in Europe, or so Tristram claimed. His specimens, which he shot, to his 'great surprise', in a dell on the south side of Mount Carmel, were a significant addition, since, until his writing, the bird had only been known by 'Antinori's unique specimen'. In *The Land of Israel,* he described the sunbird in almost voluptuous detail, no doubt aided by the two he'd shot and skinned: 'The male of Hosea's sunbird is resplendent with all the colours of the humming-bird,' he wrote, 'and not much larger than most of that tribe, measuring 4½ inches in length. It has a long, slender, and very curved bill, all the back a brilliant metallic green, the throat metallic blue, and the breast metallic purple, with a tuft of rich red, orange and yellow feathers at each shoulder (the axillary plume), which he puffs out as he hops in the trees, paying his addresses to his modestly-clad brown-green mate.'[11]

Those who obtain the first specimen of a new species often aim for posterity in their naming of it, as Tristram managed with his grackle, *onycognathus tristramii,* that orange-winged starling of the Dead Sea and Masada. But though taxonomic conventions seek to contain chaos, seek to impose order and control in their naming, they are not always successful. In the years before he died, my uncle David, an eminent entomologist, had begun to compile the first attempt at a comprehensive photographic and descriptive record and taxonomy of the insects of Israel. He kept an aquarium of unclassified coppery cockroaches he'd found, which moved so fast they almost flashed. But there were so many insect species which had not been identified or named that the unfinished work kept growing beyond his reach and control; it was a project he could never have finished. He managed something rather different with the birds of the area, which were restricted to a more manageable number; all of these he provided, for his own purposes, with a Hebrew name.

On my last day in Israel, in his house in Holon, I find his battered, dilapidated edition of the Collins bird-guide. It's the same edition that my parents have, the same as mine. I turn to page 265, bright with the purple long-tailed tit, the chestnut-coloured bearded tit, and the sunbird. 'The orange-tufted sunbird', we used to call it, though the Collins guidebook names it the 'Orange-tufted or Palestine sunbird'. It is perhaps the only bird in the entire book whose name is so politically ambivalent. The sunbird's Hebrew name is *tzofit*, a diminutive, with the same three-letter root as the word for nectar: it means something like 'little nectar bird'. In Arabic, it's called the *ta'er al nedim al Filistini*. The translation is descriptively untidy, like the bird's nest – *nedim* is a friend with whom you sit and drink wine. In Arabic, that tiny iridescent bird is therefore something like 'the Palestinian wine companion bird'; it appears on numerous Palestinian Authority stamps. In his Collins guide, my uncle has annotated the entries with Hebrew names. But on this page he has gone further, and renamed the Palestine sunbird as *tzofit ha-eretz Israel* – the 'Israeli nectar bird', or the 'nectar-bird of the Land of Israel'.

Tristram did not impose his name on the sunbird, but nor was he ambiguous about its identity: in *The Fauna and Flora of Palestine* it is named the Palestine sunbird. At the time that he shot his specimens on Mount Carmel, the bird's range was almost entirely restricted to the Jordan Valley – hence his surprise at finding them in the northwest of the country. Now the sunbird can be seen throughout Israel and the West Bank. Its growing range followed the spread of twentieth-century human settlement; it spread with the planting of urban parks and suburban and Jewish settlement gardens. But it is still unique to the area.

When I was a child we never called it the Palestine sunbird, because we never used the word Palestine. We never used the word Palestinian, either, except in passing, about terrorists. Naming acknowledges and therefore begins to validate a story. Not naming erases. *Not* naming is *tohu v'vohu* – it renders a thing void.

For me, for others like me, the name Palestine has been a bulbous, ugly nightmare creature bulging with unspoken meanings and claims, because no matter who is using the word, in what context, and no matter what particular geographical space is being designated, semantically the name Palestine erases Israel. The word makes a sort of mental noise that I cannot order or articulate, because its meaning is always ambiguous. What might it be referring to? To the West Bank, including or excluding East Jerusalem, and Gaza? To these areas and the state of Israel collectively – the latter referred to by some Palestinians, and non-Palestinians, as the '48 Lands'? Does it mean British Mandate Palestine, or Ottoman Palestine, including Transjordan, which became the Kingdom of Jordan, or a notional Palestinian state whose borders were proposed in the 1947 Partition Plan? Or does it mean a future state of Palestine along the 1949 ceasefire borders, or a future state of Palestine with borders yet to be determined? Might it be a geographical reference, or a reference to a political state?

Many passionate and ahistorical supporters of the Palestinian cause believe Israel occupies a formerly independent Palestinian state – some notional amalgam of British Mandate Palestine, Ottoman Syria, and the post-Judea province renamed Palestine by the Romans. In the popular understanding, the Jordanian and Egyptian occupation of the West Bank and Gaza from 1948 till 1967, and the thirty-two years of Britain's colonial rule preceding that, have somehow been erased.

'Palestine' presents these multiple possible meanings simultaneously, and to try to navigate them causes a kind of anxious cognitive overload – as, for a Palestinian, no doubt, do the multiple possible meanings and associations of the word 'Israel'. 'Israel' semantically erases Palestine. Like the meaning of the name Palestine, the meaning of the name Israel also changes according to context, according to who is using it. Its boundaries and evocations are similarly ambiguous: biblical Israel, Mandate Palestine, Jabotinsky's Revisionist Zionist vision of an Israel on both sides of the River Jordan... And there is the gaping semantic, historical and emotional distance between the Hebrew names *Eretz Israel*, the Land of Israel, and *Medinat Israel*, the State of Israel.

The Zionist account of the past and the present is all-encompassing: it is a total story, a comprehensive account not only of a people, but of each individual, too. To have it, to feel part of it, is to sink into the warm embrace of belonging. But to use the word Palestine or Palestinian is to lose the safety of that account. It acknowledges all the simplistic oppositions in the popular versions of the two narratives: heroic return to homeland versus European colonisation; defence against attack versus aggressive imperial expansionism; national self-determination as against racist, exclusive ethnocentrism; a war displacing people and creating refugees, or a deliberate act of ethnic cleansing. The stories are irreconcilable. To accede to part of the other is to accede to the whole, and to use the word Palestine or Palestinian is to acknowledge and therefore implicitly give credence to another narrative, a different history – and, consequently, a different set of claims. At the same time, to accede to the whole is to deny oneself a sense of place, and a past. It is safer, therefore, not to use it. Not using the word Palestine, not saying Palestine, renders that other story *tohu v'vohu* – without form, and void.

I take my uncle's battered Collin's bird-guide outside and sit in the tiny garden with a cup of coffee. I am leaving Israel again, and I don't know if I'll be coming back. The garden is full of bougainvillea, flowering pink, white and orange, and a creeper with long tube-shaped flowers that I can't identify. As the early light begins to warm the tangle of creeper over the far fence, three sunbirds appear, two males and a female. They chase each other in and out of the greenery and flowers, and one hangs gleaming and green in the fronds of a palm tree. It is close enough for me to see its curved beak, the tiny orange and yellow tufts under its shoulders, and the glistening metallic sheen of its feathers.

Orange-tufted or Palestine sunbird? I am still uneasy, but now it's for different reasons. Palestine is beginning to mean something new in popular and practical terms, with forms of official recognition and status. But if the name Palestine might now or in the near future designate a territory determined more or less along the 1949 ceasefire lines, rather than all of British Mandate Palestine, this new official meaning of the name permits a kind of cleansing of the name Israel; it allows a new level of national forgetting. All that is not-Israel can be shifted over the future border; all that is within the border can be purified of its Palestinian past, and the claims of that past; the Palestinian population of Israel can become once again an ethnic Arab minority. The Palestine sunbird can without hesitation be called the Israeli sunbird. The other story, the Palestinian story within Israel, can be at most a minority story in a nation with many minority stories. It might become a loose thread that can now be pulled out for good from the bright, finished tapestry of national history.

It is a bad sign, I think, if I can begin to use the word Palestine without discomfort and uncertainty. None of the approximations or conjoined names that attempt to repudiate that future deliberate amnesia are satisfactory – 'Israel/Palestine' or 'Israel-Palestine', or their reverse. Better that the name Palestine remain bulbous and burgeoning with ambiguity; better that the landscape remain complex and difficult; better that I hesitate between naming this tiny iridescent bird an orange-tufted sunbird, or a Palestine sunbird.

# Postscript – coming home

At home, at night after rain I lie awake in the dark listening to the river. I assess the volume of its water by the volume of its sound. Sometimes I wake at night because the sound of the river has changed. Then I get up and go downstairs and slip on my gumboots that stand ready by the door and go out into the wet night to see and feel the level of risk – will the water rise and rise, and will the stream want to break its bonds and join it here? I squelch out in the dark, everything wringing wet. Between midnight and five the village street lights are turned off, and in the summer it does not get fully dark, but even at the winter solstice it's never truly dark here, not even under heavy cloud. There is always a sense of shape in the darkness, a form to it that distinguishes object from space.

I could not ascribe to the river the usual characteristics – sullen or angry, light-hearted and singing. It is just water, squeezed into a channel. When all the streams, gullies and culverts that take the run-off from the hills and from the slopes of Mynydd Bach are emptying into it, the river slows and swells, and its surface rolls; it is brown, foamed with nitrates washed off the field where cows have stood hock-deep in its sucking muddy edges, drinking and shitting.

This is a wet place, saturated, and the water brings woe – mould, damp, creeping cold, clouds of midges, whining biteless mosquitoes and wildly accelerated growth of everything green that spreads out and clings and insinuates with roots or runners – but it also brings with it delights: the sound of the river at night, flycatchers, chittering flocks of house martins and sometimes the birds that prey on them; and, not long ago, for the first time, the evidence of an otter – its unmistakeable scale-and-fishbone scat.

It is a wet place where I live and I have been fighting it, resisting it, saying it is not my place, that I cannot bear any longer its wringing rain. But the world lives in the flow of water; we live in the flow of blood and lymph, saliva and semen and silvery secretions. We are mostly water. The lanes near here are returning to local care: the council no longer grits them in winter; the council no longer clears their ditches and culverts and drains. The civilisation we pay for is in retreat. The drains become clogged with leaves and mud from tractors churning into and out of sodden fields, ploughing or spreading muck in a near-hopeless attempt to grow something, anything, in this wet. I keep it at bay as best I can. The field above the house is turning to bog, is turning back to wild – a place that snipe come to feed; perhaps in the future curlews and lapwings will return. We are all going back to wild wet wasteland.

Three years ago, something in my body stopped and I became ill. Of course the obvious clichés had some truth, as they usually do when your body alarms you with its warning signs – about stepping back and taking stock, changing priorities, reducing stress, living a more balanced healthy life. A blood clot is a serious business, particularly a blood clot that has no clear cause. Failing to uncover its physical origins, it became a metaphor: something in me was blocked; something in me would not move on.

When I walked along the lanes here in the winter, I took a stick and redirected the blocked flow of every drain I passed, shifting the accumulated barrier of mud and grass and leaves, so that the slow water, relieved of its blockage, could flow freely again. It was not a socially responsible thing – I did it because of the fear of the blockage in me. With the blockage the flow is slowed, stopped; it spreads out and sinks; everything around it becomes waterlogged, sullen, thickly mud – and so I watched the water take up its old and proper path, beginning to flow freely, to clean the edges and surfaces, as I wished my blood to flow, cleaning the pathways of my body of its sediments, taking away loose particles, smoothing its channel as it went – towards a road-edge, a gulley, a drain; towards a stream, the river, the sea.

In the late spring, the following year, when I was better, I saw my mother again: she came to Wales to stay with me for a little while. Every woodland and garden bird was a bird my mother revelled in, as a return to something half forgotten. It had been eight years since she'd heard them – the misty early morning sound of a mistle thrush, the ticking alarm of a robin, the shrill indignation of a wren when a buzzard alighted, wet and bedraggled, in the tall sycamore. We counted off the spring migrants by sight and sound: the gently falling indeterminate song of a willow warbler, the shrieking swifts with their razor wings.

It was two weeks of birdwatching and labour, retrieving my land from wilderness that had grown through the years of neglect when my heart had been elsewhere. Together we dug and cut, weeded and planted, chose what to leave wild, what to contain – and took binoculars and went birdwatching on the coast, and along the old railway line, and in the bird reserves. But most of our birdwatching was close to home, in the garden and in the woodland, where we went walking, silent and easy together as we had been when I was a young child, in those years of innocence before we went to Israel, before Israel separated her from me.

Late in the previous year I'd asked a friend to fell eight

trees that blocked all southern and western sun, and in the spring there was light throughout the day, light inside the house, and a lifting of a dark weight that had been lying on me. In the light and space that the felling of the trees created, new birds came to visit, and to stay. Just inside the margin of the wood, loud with rain dripping off the leaves, and the fluid unbroken song of a garden warbler who seemed, from earliest light, never to stop for breath, we saw pied flycatchers. It was my mother who pointed out the female, pied brown and white with her beak full of moss, near the nest-hole high in the stem of a slender ash sapling. We stood there, very still, whispering to one another, watching them for a long time.

After the singularity of childhood, birds become more than themselves. They can never be entirely free of the stories we attach to them, the feelings and experiences we associate with them, even if we believe they give us respite from human experience, even if we believe they give back to us, for a moment, a kind of wild purity. In May, after my mother left, a pair of swallows came to visit; whenever the back door was open, they swooped around my living room: its cool interior and oak beams no doubt felt like a barn to them. Every time the door was open they came in and I had to shoo them out. One, confused, fluttered at the window and then became still, and I picked it up, holding its deep blue wings to its body. Feeling its stiff silky feathered smallness trembling, I never wanted to let it go. When I took it outside and opened my hands it launched itself from me and disappeared. But they came back, again and again, so that for a long few days I considered leaving the small window open, covering the furniture and turning the quarry-tiled room over to them for the nesting season. I didn't, in the end, but I wish I had. I hope they found somewhere else to nest; I hope they come back to my house in the spring. If they do, I'll let them in.

I watched the pied flycatchers through that summer, until they disappeared sometime in late July – watched the parents come out in the early evening to the edge of the wood and snap insects in mid-air in a flash of white, and the pair of spotted flycatchers that arrived a little later, and raised two broods. They stayed on longer, but at the end of the summer they left too. Maybe they will return – maybe they, like the swallows, will leave and return for the rest of their lives, making a home here in my home for part of the year.

Since I left Israel that last time, there has been change and no change. Terrible things have occurred: the breaking of the maritime blockade by activists; the Arab Spring followed by its long, bleak winter; the Israeli summer protests; anti-migrant violence in Tel Aviv; another war between Israel and Hamas; another election, another peace process begun and stalled; the terrible long fifty days of war in Gaza in the summer of 2014, and another election that revealed dark truths about the Prime Minister's intentions and attitudes to Israel's Arab citizens and to the right to self-determination of Palestinians. There's been the UN upgrading of Palestine's formal status, too, so that even if its borders are not clear, even if its representatives are not representatives of all Palestinians, the name Palestine becomes more clearly and singularly defined. Things change and don't change.

Usually during an upsurge in that violence, I call and email friends of mine, and members of my family – a man from Gaza City whose family I once met in Cardiff, Eitan in Be'er Sheva, my aunts and uncle. But recently I've done that less and less. I have been back, in the quiet after Operation Protective Edge, to research another book, and I know I'll go back again – maybe this year, maybe next. Each time I'm afraid of what will happen when I do: I'm afraid of reawakening that intensity, all that feeling – more feeling than I want, and the uncertainty it brings. But it's where my mother's from, it's where my grandparents and great-grandparents are buried, and so the place won't ever let me be, not entirely.

The Welsh philosopher J.R. Jones described, hauntingly, 'the experience of knowing, not that you are leaving your country, but that your country is leaving you, is ceasing to exist under your very feet, is being sucked away from you, as if by an insatiable, consuming wind'. He was lamenting the loss of a unique way of life and shared experience which was being strangled out of existence, grieving for a language that was being depleted and silenced. His was a call for 'the struggle of the conquered for their very existence, the struggle to save their identity from being trampled into oblivion'.[12]

My country Israel is leaving me too, but not 'into the hands and possession of another country and another civilization', as J.R. Jones saw the predicament of Wales, and as is the predicament of Palestine. My country is leaving me because its story is ceasing to exist, and because of what it has strangled out of existence. I grieve the loss, I grieve its departure from me, but it's a grief coloured darkly by shame.

This is the longest I've been in one place since I left home at seventeen and went to Israel. Is this how it happens,  ·

settling down – without you really noticing? You believe it is a displacement of another love; you believe it is love on the rebound, but it settles into something new; you love despite yourself. 'One is trying to make a shape out of the very things of which one is oneself made', the poet and artist David Jones observed in his careful, distancing description of his work – himself making out of an imagined Palestine and a lived experience as a soldier in 1917 a new Welsh and Catholic mythos; but he might also have said that one makes a new self, too, out of those things one has made.[13]

When it rains hard, the stream they put under the field will try again to find its old way. It won't stay, and the field won't take it, so it will burst out of the pipes and pour down the wadi it has made out of the rock, a gulley too narrow and shallow to hold it. This is the way it wants to flow, and perhaps I can let it – perhaps I can stop resisting, and make a place for this water, just as perhaps I can stop resisting, and accept that I have made a place here for myself. Perhaps I will name the stream and put it on the map. All the lanes and roads in Wales lead in the end to what were once secret and illicit chapels named after Hebron and Jerusalem and Pisgah, after Zion; around the chapels grew hamlets of the same name, and then villages. Perhaps I will name it not Nant y Moch, Pig Stream, though it runs past an old ruined pig house, but a Hebrew name, according to the tradition of this place: Nant Gilboa, where the black irises grow above the Jezreel Valley, overlooking Beit Hashita, where my heart has been.

Love of a person, of a place – the more you know, the more complicated it is. The knowledge that the person is wounded, that the place is stained doesn't diminish your love. The person and the place matter less, perhaps, than your need to love, and your need to love is a longing to feel whole, knowing you cannot be whole – a longing to be home, though you will never be at home in one place, not fully.

# Notes

1. Yehuda Amichai, 'Jerusalem is full of used Jews', *The Selected Poetry of Yehuda Amichai*, trans. Chana Bloch and Stephen Mitchell (New York: HarperPerennial, 1992), p. 135.

2. Tsfarir Corcia, 'War of Words on the streets of Tel Aviv', www.ynetnews.com, 8 August 2006.

3. Bayard Taylor, *The Lands of the Saracen* (1855); John Mills, *Palestina* (1858); Mark Twain, *The Innocents Abroad* (American Publishing Company, 1869), p. 520.

4. H.B. Tristram, *The Land of Israel: a Journal of Travel with Reference to its Physical History* (1865), p. 500.

5. H.B. Tristram, *Bible Places or, The Topography of the Holy Land* (1875), p. 239.

6. Amia Lieblich, *Kibbutz Makom* (London: Andre Deutsch, 1982), p. 23. The following quotes by Saul are from pp. 18-23.

7. Emile Habiby, *The Secret Life of Saeed the Pessoptomist* (Northampton, MA: Interlink, 2003), p. 127.

8. Karl Sabbagh, *Palestine, a Personal Story* (New York: Grove Press, 2007), p. 79.

9. Walid Khalidi (ed.), *All That Remains: the Palestinian Villages Occupied and Depopulated by Israel in 1948* (Washington: Institute for Palestine Studies, 1996), p. 55.

10. Rahel, 'With my own hands'. There's a slightly different translation in *Flowers of Perhaps: Selected Poems of Ra'hel*, trans. Robert Friend (London: The Menard Press, 1994), p. 51.

11. H.B. Tristram, *The Land of Israel* (1876), p. 199.

12. J.R. Jones, *Gwaedd yng Nghymru* (1970), published in

translation in Meic Stephens (ed.), *A Book of Wales* (London: J. M. Dent, 1987), p. 157.

13. David Jones, Preface to *The Anathemata,* in *Selected Works of David Jones*, ed. John Matthias (Cardiff: University of Wales Press, 1992), p.116.

# A note on sources

On the contested nature of what happened between 1947 and 1949, the two poles of the 'new history' are Ilan Pappe and Benny Morris. Avi Shlaim's many publications, and publications by Walid Khalidi and others also help illustrate the difficulty of interpreting the evidence. Benny Morris's views before and after 2000 have been the subject of much discussion. See, for example, Ari Shavit's interview with him, 'Survival of the Fittest? An interview with Benny Morris', in *Ha'aretz* on 8 January 2004.

For Joan Peters's unreconstructed Zionist view of the history, see her volume *From Time Immemorial*, and Alan Dershowitz's use of her findings, for which Norman Finkelstein attacked him in a notorious exchange that raked over the dubious reportage of Mark Twain and other nineteenth-century Western travellers. See for example Norman Finkelstein, *Beyond Chutzpah: On the Misuse of Anti-Semitism and the Abuse of History* (Berkeley: University of California Press, 2008), and extensive material on his website, www.normanfinkelstein.com.

There are many sources for village statistics, including Walid Khalidi's *All That Remains,* and Benny Morris's *The Birth of the Palestinian Refugee Problem*. The figures vary. Historians' population statistics are based on projections from British surveys, including the Census of Palestine in 1931. The website www.palestineremembered.com includes extensive material, including oral history interviews in Arabic. On the question of Arab 'collaboration', see

Hillel Cohen's *Army of Shadows: Palestinian Collaboration with Zionism, 1917-1948* (Berkeley: University of California Press, 2008).

A great deal has been written on the kibbutz experiment. Melford Spiro's *Children of the Kibbutz* was an important volume, and in addition to Amia Lieblich's *Kibbutz Makom* I relied on Avraham Balaban, *Mourning a Father Lost: a Kibbutz Childhood Remembered* (Lanham: Rowman and Littlefield, 2004), Daniel Gavron, *The Kibbutz: Awakening from Utopia* (Lanham: Rowman and Littlefield, 2000) and Naama Sabar, *Kibbutzniks in the Diaspora* (Albany: SUNY, 2000).

For autobiographical and fictional works exploring the Palestinian experience see, for example, Mourid Barghouti's *I Saw Ramallah* (London: Bloomsbury, 2004), Raja Shehadeh's *Palestinian Walks: Notes on a Vanishing Landscape* (London: Profile, 2008), Suad Amiry, *Sharon and My Mother-in-Law: Ramallah Diaries* (New York: Anchor, 2006), and Samir El-Youssef's *The Illusion of Return* (London: Halban, 2008). For fictional treatment of Israeli-Arab experience see Sayed Kashua's *Dancing Arabs* (New York: Grove, 2002) and Emile Habiby's *The Secret Life of Saeed the Pessoptomist* (Northampton: Interlink, 2003). For Arab-Jewish experience, see Rachel Shabi's *We Look Like the Enemy: the Hidden Story of Israel's Jews from Arab Lands* (New York: Walker and Co, 2008).

The map referred to in Chapter 2 is in the possession of Zochrot.

Some individuals' names are pseudonyms.

# Works cited

Abu Sitta, Salman. *Atlas of Palestine 1948* (London: Palestine Land Society, 2005).

——, *The Return Journey: A Guide* (London: Palestine Law Society, 2007).

Amichai, Yehuda. *The Selected Poetry of Yehuda Amichai*, trans. Chana Bloch and Stephen Mitchell (New York: HarperPerennial, 1992).

Habiby, Emile. *The Secret Life of Saeed the Pessoptomist* (Northampton, MA: Interlink, 2003).

Heinzel, Hermann, Richard Fitter and John Parslow. *The Birds of Britain and Europe, with North Africa and the Middle East* (London: Collins, 1972).

Jones, David. *Selected Works of David Jones*, ed. John Matthias (Cardiff: University of Wales Press, 1992).

Jones, J.R. *Gwaedd yng Nghymru* (Lerpwl: Cyhoeddiadau Modern Cymreig, 1970).

Khalidi, Walid (ed.). *All That Remains: the Palestinian Villages Occupied and Depopulated by Israel in 1948* (Washington: Institute for Palestine Studies, 1996).

Lieblich, Amia. *Kibbutz Makom: Report from an Israeli Kibbutz* (London: Andre Deutsch, 1982).

Mills, John. *Palestina: sef Hanes Taith i Ymweld ag Iuddewon Gwlad Canaan* (1858).

——, *Three Months' Residence at Nablus, and an Account of the Modern Samaritans* (1864).

Morris, Benny. *The Birth of the Palestinian Refugee Problem* (Cambridge: Cambridge University Press, 1987).

Or, Amir. *Poem*, trans. Helena Berg (Dublin: Dedalus Press, 2004).

Pappe, Ilan. *The Ethnic Cleansing of Palestine* (Oxford: Oneworld, 2006).

Peters, Joan. *From Time Immemorial* (New York: Harper and Row, 1984).

Rahel, *Flowers of Perhaps: Selected Poems of Ra'hel*, trans. Robert Friend (London: The Menard Press, 1994).

Sabbagh, Karl. *Palestine, a Personal Story* (New York: Grove Press, 2007).

Salamon, Ya'acov. *In My Own Way* (Haifa: Gillie Salomon Foundation, 1982).

Spiro, Melford. *Children of the Kibbutz: A Study in Child Training and Personality* (1958; Cambridge: Harvard University Press, 1975).

Stein, Kenneth. *The Land Question in Palestine, 1917-1939* (Chapel Hill: University of North Carolina Press, 1984).

Stephens, Meic (ed.). *A Book of Wales* (London: J.M. Dent, 1987).

Taylor, Bayard. *The Lands of the Saracen or, Pictures of Palestine, Asia Minor, Sicily, and Spain* (1855).

Tristram, H.B. *The Fauna and Flora of Palestine* (1884).

——, *The Land of Israel* (1876).

——, *Bible Places, or, The Topography of the Holy Land* (1875).

——, *The Topography of the Holy Land* (1872).

——, *The Land of Israel: a Journal of Travel with Reference to its Physical History* (1865).

Twain, Mark. *The Innocents Abroad* (1869).

Uris, Leon. *Exodus* (New York: Doubleday, 1958).

——, *The Haj* (New York: Doubleday, 1984).

Wright, James. *Above the River* (New York: The Noonday Press, 1992).

## Websites

www.palestineremembered.org
www.palyam.org
www.zochrot.org

## Other works consulted and further reading

Adonis, Mahmud Darwish and Samih al-Qasim, *Victims of a Map: A Bilingual Anthology of Arabic Poetry* (1984; London: Saqi, 2005).

Amiry, Suad. *Sharon and My Mother-in-Law: Ramallah Diaries* (New York: Anchor, 2006).

Anglim, Simon. *Orde Wingate, The Iron Wall and Counter-Terrorism in Palestine 1937-1939* (The Strategic and Combat Studies Institute, Occasional Papers: 2005).

Balaban, Avraham. *Mourning a Father Lost: a Kibbutz Childhood Remembered* (Lanham, Maryland: Rowman and Littlefield, 2004).

Barghouti, Mourid. *I Saw Ramallah* (London: Bloomsbury, 2004).

Board, Barbara. *Reporting From Palestine 1943-1944* (Nottingham: Five Leaves, 2008).

Cohen, Hillel. *Army of Shadows: Palestinian Collaboration with Zionism, 1917-1948* (Berkeley: University of California Press, 2008).

Collins, Norman J. and Anton Steichele. *The Ottoman Post and Telegraph Offices in Palestine and Sinai* (London: Sahara, 2000).

Darwish, Mahmoud. *Unfortunately, It Was Paradise: Selected Poems* (Berkeley: University of California Press, 2003).

El-Youssef, Samir. *The Illusion of Return* (London: Halban, 2008).

Finkelstein, Norman. *The Holocaust Industry: Reflections on the Exploitation of Jewish Suffering* (London: Verso, 2000).
——, *Beyond Chutzpah: On the Misuse of Anti-Semitism and the Abuse of History* (Berkeley: University of California Press, 2008).

Freedman, Seth. *Can I Bring My Own Gun: An Israeli Soldier's Story* (Nottingham: Five Leaves/ GuardianBooks, 2009).

Garfinkel, Jonathan. *Ambivalence: Crossing the Israel/Palestine Divide* (London: Saqi, 2007).

Gavron, Daniel. *The Kibbutz: Awakening from Utopia* (Lanham, Maryland: Rowman and Littlefield, 2000).

Grossman, David. *To the End of the Land* (London: Jonathan Cape, 2010).

Kashua, Sayed. *Dancing Arabs* (New York: Grove, 2002).

Khalidi, Rashid. *The Iron Cage: the Story of the Palestinian Struggle for Statehood* (2006; Oxford: Oneworld, 2009).

LeBor, Adam. *City of Oranges: Arabs and Jews in Jaffa* (London: Bloomsbury, 2006).

Marqusee, Mike. *If I Am Not For Myself: Journey of an anti-Zionist Jew* (London: Verso, 2008).

Nicholson, James. *The Hejaz Railway* (London: Stacey International, 2005).

Nimni, Ephraim (ed.). *The Challenge of Post-Zionism: Alternatives to Israeli Fundamentalist Politics* (London: Zed Books, 2003).

Oz, Amos. *A Tale of Love and Darkness* (London: Chatto & Windus, 2004).

Pappe, Ilan (ed.). *The Israel/Palestine Question: Rewriting Histories* (London: Routledge, 1999).

Rogan, Eugene L. and Avi Shlaim. *The War for Palestine: Rewriting the History of 1948* (Cambridge: Cambridge University Press, 2001).

Sabar, Naama. *Kibbutzniks in the Diaspora* (Albany, NY: SUNY, 2000).

Sand, Shlomo. *The Invention of the Jewish People* (London: Verso, 2009).

Segev, Tom. *One Palestine, Complete: Jews and Arabs under the British Mandate* (London: Abacus, 2001).

Shabi, Rachel. *We Look Like the Enemy: the Hidden Story of Israel's Jews from Arab Lands* (New York: Walker and Co, 2008).

Shavit, Ari. 'Survival of the Fittest? An interview with Benny Morris', 8 January 2004, www.haaretz.com/survival-of-the-fittest-1.61345.

Shehadeh, Raja. *Palestinian Walks: Notes on a Vanishing Landscape* (London: Profile, 2008).

Shepherd, Naomi. *Ploughing Sand: British Rule in Palestine 1917-1948* (London: John Murray, 1999).

Shlaim, Avi. *The Iron Wall: Israel and the Arab World* (London: Penguin, 2000).

# Acknowledgements

This book was a long time in the making (and remaking) and I am grateful to Literature Wales for a writer's bursary in 2009, which supported part of the work. My thanks to members of my family, particularly my aunts, my uncle and my cousins, who helped and supported me with warm and welcoming hospitality, contacts, suggestions, discussion and encouragement, even when we did not necessarily agree. Thank you also to Ghaith, Randa, and Jasr Al Kawkuby for help, hospitality and friendship, and to staff members at Zochrot for information and contacts.

Nemonie Craven helped shape an early draft of this book and I am grateful to her for her enthusiasm about the project. My thanks to friends who encouraged me, particularly to Wynn Thomas and Jem Poster, who saw early versions. My thanks also to Mick Felton for helping me fine-tune the final text. Most importantly, I am grateful to my dear friend Helgard Krause for a characteristically acerbic piece of criticism: without it, this book would not have been published.

# A note on the author

Jasmine Donahaye's books include a biography, *The Greatest Need: the Creative Life and Troubled Times of Lily Tobias, A Welsh Jew in Palestine* (2015); the cultural study *Whose People? Wales, Israel, Palestine* (2012), and two poetry collections, *Misappropriations* (2006) and *Self-Portrait as Ruth* (2009).